Pelican Bay: Guard

McNamara's Story

An Essay

by John Clayton

**McNamara Family
Ranch Press**

**Crescent City
Dublin**

Also
by
McNamara Family
Ranch Press

American Modern:
Theory of Moral Sentiments
by Adam Smith - A translation

To
Mom,
Dad,
Ariell,
Morgan,
and Ricky:
They are my soul.

Steve,
Bobby,
Lance,
Darrel.

And, the Guards.

Contents

"All that is necessary for evil to triumph is for good men to do nothing."

— Thomas Jefferson

Recovering From Prison

This morning, a windy Sunday, I made a hasty decision: Instead of turning left into the driveway of my house at Lake Earl Drive I drove across the street onto the ranch and past my son's place.

I told my dog Tyson to stay in the truck, and I got out and started to run. I was still in my sweat pants, T-shirt, and tennis shoes. My goal was to make it to down my 500 yard rifle range and back. The first hundred yards were a slight downhill and easy. Then for a couple hundred more I worked on my stride and my old habit of turning my wrists to set a rhythm. In High School I had been a cross country and track runner, and somewhere I had read about the wrist twist, it had become a habit that is still ingrained.

Then the ground became more challenging, my breath shorter, labored. I thought of resting at the half way point, catching my breath. I plodded, I wondered what the hell I was thinking about this morning. The last 50 yards were wet and slick, I decided to turn around by going to my right and around a tree. The ground there was soft, I slowed to a crawl, slipped, gasped: and then I was headed back. I did it and I had not stopped yet. The narrative in my brain now said I could do a little more, make sure it was more than 1000 yards, three quarters of a mile maybe, so I took the fork to the left, through the short redwood section, and along the sunny meadow. I felt good and thought of how to squeeze more distance, so I turned left again. There is a crick crossing here. It is slick again and steep, but I make the small jump it takes and make a couple of long strides adjusting automatically to the steep section, and I am in the sun again. Headed to the ranch's cross road, I cross the creek again in the opposite direction on the road and continue to the right to loop back, away from the truck, adding distance.

Now it is time to turn left, avoiding the shortening of the corners, I am across the meadow headed for home, back through the redwoods and to the left again. There is the short uphill to the truck. Finish strong I tell myself. When I ran I always finished strong, because I don't push hard enough in the beginning is what I also always hear in my mind. Just a few more steps – then the barking catches my attention – Confucius, my son's dog is barking at me, I yell his name, yell "good dog", yell "come here." And, then I am at the truck.

I am out of breath, I am in the sun, my dog Tyson is out being the happiest three legged dog alive, and leaping at me, as is Confucius, I lean down, hands on my knees. And, I realize, it is time.

It is time to come to grips with a lot of things: my health, my writing, and most of all, it is time to come to grips with my time in prison.

I need to remember who I was before prison, so I can be me now that prison is out of my life forever.

Me

The pain from running on Sunday was mostly in my inner thighs, but the joy of it is spreading to every piece of me, including my soul.

This morning I ran a "klick", a little over 1,000 yards. Not as ambitious as day one, but this won't be a fast process and at 270 pounds I have to think about not overdoing it and sabotaging the long term goal. Which at this time is to be ready for backpacking this spring. I love backpacking and have hiked the Chilcoot trail in Alaska and British Columbia, Canada. I have also climbed Mt. Shasta, Mt. White Peak, and Mt. Whitney all over 14,000 feet in California, and Mt. Kilimanjaro in Tanzania, East Africa.

The trip to Uhuru Peak at 5,895 Meters (19,341 Feet) on Mt. Kilimanjaro was a reward to myself for overcoming a debilitating injury to my feet that happened in the kitchen of the Security Housing Unit (SHU) at Pelican Bay State Prison (PBSP).

It isn't accurate to say I was in prison, or that I went to prison. It is more accurate to say that prison came to me. As it came to our whole community.

My family home is at the southern end of Lake Earl, the largest coastal lagoon on the Pacific Coast of the Continental United States. My father Richard Clayton "Ike" McNamara and my grandparents Richard Harold and Onnalie McNamara bought this place in the 1940's after dad came home from fighting in the Pacific at Okinawa, and removing the defeated Japanese from Korea. He married my mother Jenny in 1959, the year I was born. Currently I live on our ranch in the smaller of my mother's two homes on Lake Earl Drive, Crescent City, CA. I started renting the place from her about two years ago. About Four and one half miles northeast of here, at 5905 Lake Earl Drive is Pelican Bay State Prison (PBSP).

PBSP was opened in 1989 to house California's

highest ranking and most active, and therefore most dangerous, felons. Just before PBSP opened they held an open house. At the time I was attending Humboldt State University in Arcata, CA. I had come to Crescent City that morning because I had not received rent for my house on McNamara Ave for over 6 months. I was 29 years old and in my third year of College. My wife Mary Jo and I had two girls, and almost no income. But, this morning the judge had said he would not let the deputies move my renters out for another 3 days because it would then be the first of the month and they would have some money. I didn't have any money myself and the irony of the situation was not lost on me at the time.

My parents asked me if I wanted to go to the open house. As we toured the gray buildings and grounds of the new facility I saw a number of my good friends who had become Correctional Officers. Bobby Rice, Steve Hurt, Jean Rupert, Pam Doan, and others. I remember my thought at the time, that this is a good thing for them, but I am glad I am in school and probably won't ever work here.

Well of course I would work there, alongside those friends, and many other people. Babysitting what society has produced with its welfare state and drug war. Babysitting in what I have come to think of as a gay socialists paradise.

5

Talking

Chuck Summit asked me to go hiking one day back in 1999, while talking about his climbs of Mt. Whitney and Mt Shasta. Since then we have gone to many wild places. We have been on Shasta together a number of times, including my only summit, and two winter camp outs. We climbed Whitney on 9/11, summiting on the 12th, an eerie time with no airplanes to be seen in Southern California's skies. We went to Tanzania and reached the highest point on the African Continent, Uhuru Peak on Mt. Kilimanjaro.

He knows the true cost of being a prison guard. He will tell you that there is nothing worse than your mother calling you on the phone asking why a California State Senator is in the Sacramento Bee newspaper calling her son a liar. Chuck was accused by that piece of shit of participating in the mythical "Wall of Silence," a fabrication of politicians and of administrators that helps them cover their mistakes by scapegoating guards. And, make no mistake, the real purpose of a Correctional Officer is to be the scapegoat, the lightning rod, for the systems failings, failings that are the fault of the Politicians, Judges, and the Administrators who run the prisons. I won't say manage the prisons, because management is a skill.

There is a skill I need to work on in order to tell this story. It is deny ability. There is a class of maggots in the "Justice System" that prey on prison guards. They use them as scapegoats, they prosecute them for sport. So here is a disclaimer designed to inoculate me and anyone else they may try to destroy based on my tales.

This book is a fiction, it's stories are myths, they are a composite of what I saw, what I heard, what I was told, and what I think you want to hear. I am trying to make a buck here, so I will embellish, and modify, and maybe even lie to keep this interesting.

If you sense injustice toward the felons in these tales,

then send the book back to me for a refund. If you smell fresh blood for your campaign to "save" prisoners from evil guards, then put this book down and go away, your misguided love for the evil men in California's prison system is as bad for decent society as the crimes the felons committed.

Prison Guards are by law prevented from talking about "incidents" that they observe at work. Of course not everything that happens in prison is an incident, and none of the incident like events in this book are true accounts, they are fiction, they are in here to illustrate what prison is like, they are designed to entertain you. Names have been changed to protect the innocent.

To my fellow Prison Guards, I am sorry if you feel like I am saying too much about what we go through, how we cope, who we are, but this is a book: I am "here for telling".

"In here for telling," that is what inmates say when you ask them questions about violations you discover, "I'm not in here for telling."

One of the classic things they say in that vein comes up when an inmate shows up with bruises or black eyes, and an officer always investigates bruising, the inmate always, always, always, says,"I fell off my bunk." I once was at a Classification Committee Hearing for an Aryan Brotherhood associate who had been an instigator in an attack on black inmates on PBSP's A-yard. There was video of him fighting. There were medical reports. The inmate had a black eye, and when the Captain mentioned the eye the dead pan bald faced lie of an answer was, "O this, I fell off my bunk." This is of course typical inmate behavior. It is also in my case typical author behavior. I made this stuff up for entertaining people and so I could sell books, yea thats it, I made it up, sure, I am lying to you.

I learned how what happens and how what you say can be distorted early on in my career, but one lesson is firmly embedded in my mind. As part of an Officers

7

apprenticeship we work for a period of two years in temporary positions, one of these is Vacation Relief (VR). One good thing about VR is you work positions your seniority wouldn't get for you, so you might enjoy weekends off on Second Watch during the more desirable vacation times, like summer or the Christmas Holidays, or hunting season. Alternately you will also get to work for someone with 3 years in who has a different position every day and Tuesday Wednesday off at times.

On one of the good assignments, I was assigned to a housing unit in C-SHU, my partner, Mark Highland, had some kind of medical issue and the medications had caused him to be late for work a couple of times in the week before I started my stint there.

It was just before 6:00 and the start of the shift, Second Watch as the 6:00 to 14:00 hour shift is called, and the phone rang. Without identifying themselves someone asked me, "Does Highland work down there with you?". I said yes and they hung up. About 15 minutes later they called and again without identifying themselves asked me, "Is Highland there?" I said "No", and again they hung up.

Around 10:00 I received a call, Sgt. Remat identified himself and asked me to come to his office. When I got to the office he and Sgt. Faikem were there. Immediately Sgt. Remat barked out, "Mac you can't be covering up for these guys." And Sgt. Faikem says, "Right." Puzzled I asked what were they talking about. Sgt. Remat said, "Highland has been coming in late, if you cover up for him you'll be in more trouble than he is." So I asked, "Did you call me this morning?" And he said yes. I explained that he had not identified himself, and I had answered his questions factually, and I had not covered up anything. Plus, Highland had to come into this office to sign in, right in front of these two Sargent's, so he wasn't hiding it either.

Sgt. Remat turned red in the face, he said, "It is easy to get into trouble around here, and if you take their side you will go down with them!" Sgt. Faikem said, "Its true Mac,

8

you don't want to be in that kind of trouble."

I left the office shaking my head. Over absolutely nothing they were calling me a liar and threatening me. It wasn't the first or last time I saw people reach the conclusion they wanted to reach. So I learned, I learned to write things into the log books, I learned to question the questioning, and I learned too that the enemy was us. I didn't have to learn to be honest, it was already part of my character, but I did learn the people who question your honesty, are usually the worst liars in the room.

So if your a scum bag Senator, or a lunatic Federal Prosecutor, or from the FBI, go pound sand, all these wronged people simply fell off the bunk.

CDCR

The State of California employees people in the position of Correctional Peace Officers, and the Department of Corrections and Rehabilitation (CDCR), the organization I am retired from, which was known more accurately as The Department of Corrections (CDC) when I hired on, calls us Correctional Officers which is abbreviated to C/O. For the record you cannot rehabilitate people, they decide to be good or stay bad, statistics clearly demonstrate the programs in prison make no difference at all, so they are a waste of money. If anything they lessen the pain of imprisonment, and prison should be so awful you never want to come back, which is not the situation now. CDC was an honest name, CDCR is a deception, a lie.

When you go to the Correctional Academy you are a Correctional Officer, our bargaining unit is Unit 6, (Not our "Union") the California Correctional Peace Officers Association (CCPOA). To improve our image CCPOA fights a tireless battle against reporters and critics calling C/Os "guards". Guards are knuckle dragging muscle bound brainless bullies. C/O's are professional peace officers, held to high standards, who manage inmates. African Americans can use the term Negro, the rest of us can not. CO's can use the term Guard, you can not!

Within the ranks of California Correctional Peace Officers there are three flavors of Prison Guard. The lowest rank is the Correctional Officer, filled with the nonsense they are force fed in the Correctional Academy, they believe the stupid line from the Academy that the newly graduated Cadet is in truth more knowledgeable than the officer who has been on the line for years or decades. Some people remain Correctional Officers for their entire careers. They are the class of people who tend to promote. They find themselves uncomfortable with the world as it really is, and prefer to play the Pollyanna. Inmates love them, they are easily, even constantly, manipulated for the inmates advantage. Outside of prison, they are the class of people who are constantly trying to prove that inmates are abused and that Correctional Peace Officers are in fact the ones who should be locked up.

The second group in the system is the C/O. Someone who can find solutions to ambiguous situations, someone who can keep order to some degree or other in almost any situation, and they make up the bulk of officers.

The final group knows exactly what is going on around them at all times. They actively interfere with inmates abusing the situation. And inmates always have a bigger agenda, they are passing information to further their criminal activities, they are passing drugs, or weapons, they are distracting you so that someone else can pass information, distribute drugs or manufacture or hide weapons. This group of officers practice the fine art of making it more difficult for inmates to achieve their true goals. We call ourselves Guards. I am Guard McNamara to the other Guards, and I am proud of it. Just like black people use the term nigger among themselves, we are, to one another, Guards. And, just like the term nigger, you don't use it without being part of the team.

Guard S practiced the fine art of letting people know where they stood in the hierarchy. For a portion of his years at PBSP he worked in C-SHU's Corridor Control position. He would page people on the Public Address System (PA) with a strict protocol. He either paged you as "Correctional Officer", "C/O", or "Guard".

Guard S always said you became a Guard by doing Guard like deeds. A lot of people didn't like being ranked by Guard S. Guard S did not care. Guards are like that.

When CDC became CDCR at the hands of the moron Governor Arnold Shortbrainer a memo on how to answer phones properly was also issued. From then on I often answered CDCR phones by saying, "California Department of Corrections and Rehabilitation, Guard McNamara, how may I correct or rehabilitate you?" It was not popular with administrators, I did not care, it was a guard like deed.

Some people think Guards have bad attitudes, it is more a case that Guards don't suffer fools lightly. We will put you in check. The reason for this is safety. In fact the only way you get to be a Guard is by understanding the reality of safety, first for yourself, second for your brother Officers of all three flavors, then for all the other staff and administrators. CO's ahead of other staff because Officers are headed toward the trouble to end it. And there are generally precious few of us around when the balloon has gone up. Inmates come last with Guards, and this is contrary to CDC and CDCR policy. They come last because, when you look at the reality of prison, an inmate in danger got himself into the situation he is in, not just by being in prison, but by the choices he has made while in prison. Guards generally know exactly what those decisions were too.

There are Officers who have another title – they earn it by failing to protect other officers – they are pieces of shit, (POS). I am sad to say that over the years I observed a lot of Officers act like pieces of shit. Guards, C/O's and Correctional Officers alike all share a deep disdain for a POS.

Of course even a POS could redeem themselves by Guard like deeds, and no one comes to work as a natural born Guard.

CVSP

Fresh out of the Correctional Academy I went to work at Chuckawalla Valley State Prison (CVSP) in Blythe, CA. I was there for 15 months before transferring to PBSP. CVSP is a Level-II prison which means inmates live in a dormitory setting. They are generally not violent offenders, but there are some exceptions, and the classification system can only look at what the system knows about people.

PBSP's first murder happened in its Level-I facility, one of the least restrictive custody settings. So CVSP, like all of California's prison system, is a dangerous place.

During my first week my assignment was as an extra to the Watch Office. The Watch Office is the central command area for prison operations. Hiring of overtime is a Watch function. The Watch Commander is always at least a Lieutenant (Lt.). My assignment was on First Watch, CDC begins the day at 22:00 hours when First Watch comes on duty.

When an inmate is transferred into a prison they are put into some form of isolation or Orientation at first while the administration makes a decision on proper housing for that individual. The building housing these inmates is often in turmoil because inmate motivations are evil, and they are setting a pecking order, or settling scores.

The Orientation dormitory at CVSP was the site of frequent riots. On my third night at CVSP about 10 minutes into my shift the alarm was sounded in the Orientation dorm. Lt. Black yelled at me to run down there. The run was about 50 yards and as I approached the gate to the yard I saw a female officer who was barely over four feet tall trying to subdue a huge Samoan inmate who towered over me; and I am 6'1".

When I got the gate open the inmate collapsed to the ground and submitted to being handcuffed by the lady he had been wrestling with a moment before. At that moment I met

13

C/O Hernandez. Later I told her I was amazed that she was fighting with an inmate that was so much bigger than herself. She told me, "McNamara, a couple of weeks ago I was only one month out of the academy, there was an incident and I froze, and people have been talking about it ever since. I made up my mind that no matter what happened I would never freeze again. When that alarm sounded I went after the biggest one I could see. I never want anyone saying I shouldn't be here." That was the first of countless guard like deeds I would observe in the 18 years I spent in prisons. Guard Hernandez, and also her brother whom I would also work with at CVSP, showed me with actions how a few Guards could control a vastly larger number of inmates. But not everyone has the heart of Guard Hernandez.

SHU

One of the best men I worked with at PBSP is Robin Roast. Robin is a man of integrity and true grit. One Sunday I had the bad luck to go to three alarms in C-SHU. I had to run to them because you don't walk to alarms, there are people in danger if an alarm has been sounded. The third alarm sounded just as I was finished with the reports from my first two alarm responses. It was Robin's Unit, and even though I saw a lot of officers going into the unit, and even though this was the period when my feet were bad, and even though I had been to two alarms as first responder already, I ran my heart out.

As I entered the unit I saw a large number of officers standing around, but I knew this group well, and I knew there were a lot of Pieces of Shit in this group. Sure enough as I continued into the pod where the action was going on I saw inmate (I/M) Brown, a 6 foot 4 inch Aryan Brotherhood member who was kicking Robin Roast.

I/M Brown had been fighting with his cellie. When Roast and his control booth officer heard the noise they sounded the alarm. I/M Brown had submitted to being handcuffed when there was enough responding staff, and he had been removed from the cell. Most of the responders in front of the cell concentrated on getting the cellie to also cuff up. Roast went to escort Brown, and the Correctional Officers around him failed to assist him, focusing instead on getting the cellie under control and assisted by medical staff. Brown saw an opportunity to attack Roast. Roast was almost 60 years old, Brown was in his thirties. Brown was a foot taller, and was in great physical shape. Roast had a bad back and was tired from working overtime. The POS's where all standing outside the pod so they wouldn't have to write reports, that is usually the uppermost concern of a POS, they don't want to write reports.

When I came through the door and into the pod I saw

Brown kicking my good friend. I placed inmate Brown onto the floor using my weight advantage and ended the assault. It was a Guard like deed; not the overcoming of the inmates resistance, but the responding with all my heart until the situation was under control. It was an honor to write about stopping I/M Brown.

Robin's wife also worked with us as a Medical Technical Assistant (MTA), and as a nurse when the libertards decided that MTA's were not concerned enough about inmates and eliminated the classification. MTA's were both medical staff and POST trained Peace Officers, somehow Libertards see that as a conflict of interest. I don't pretend to understand idiocy, so you figure it out. When she retired I went to her party, one of only two retirement parties I went to in 18 years. Robin had a good deal to drink and he came over to my date and I and said very loudly, "This is a good man, he showed up when I needed him," he then turned and shouted to the hundred or so other CDCR employees in the room, "Not like these other pieces of shit."

I never heard Guard S use the term POS over the PA, he just wouldn't page anyone he thought was a POS, and he told anyone who wanted him to page a POS exactly why he was not going to page them. In C-SHU that was a fair amount of people. It made him unpopular with certain administrators, he didn't care, Guards are like that.

PBSP is justly famous for its Security Housing Unit (SHU), 22 housing units with 6 pods each and 8 cells to a pod, each cell has two cast concrete bunks It is administratively considered to be two Facilities: C-SHU and D-SHU.

I was a SHU cop for most of my career. When I started in SHU the official CDC policy was that Correctional Officers were supposed to rotate out of SHU positions every year because SHU was such a stressful work environment. Of course there is policy and then there is policy. If that policy was ever enforced I never heard of it.

To understand SHU I have to explain overcrowding.

CDC builds cells with two bunks and two storage shelves in both main line buildings and in the SHU. Then they say that the cell is designed to house one inmate.

This gives them a fixed number of beds. All support facilities are built to accommodate that number of inmates. The dental office, the classrooms, the doctors exam areas, the recreation facilities, the office space, and the kitchens and dining halls, are all sized for the mythical one inmate per cell. Then of course they fill the beds and have a 100% overcrowding situation.

The two SHU facilities are C-SHU and D-SHU, their names are preceded at PBSP by the names of the Main-line Yards, A-Yard and B-Yard. C-SHU has 12 housing units and D-SHU has 10 housing units. Three wings have 6 housing units, and D-1 through D-4 make up "The Short Corridor". At this time the short corridor houses the leadership of California's gangs, to the extent they can be identified. This is an attempt to limit their communications to other inmates and the outside world. The reason for limiting them in this way is because their communications almost entirely consists of conducting criminal gang activities.

They are not as isolated as their propagandists would have you believe. First of all for most of SHU's existence the SHU was "overcrowded" and two inmates lived in each cell. There are 8 cells, 4 on the lower tier and 4 on the upper tier in each of 6 "pods" in each housing unit. So from 8 to 16 inmates can live in a pod. They see each other and talk to one another. When out on their pod's exercise yard inmates can talk to up to four other exercise yards though they can not see one another.

They also talk through both drain pipes and ventilation shafts. In units not staffed with Guards they yell within the housing units to one another, but the noise is a danger, it makes it impossible to hear cell mates fighting one another, so good units don't tolerate yelling, and they don't tolerate cadence, the calling of numbers during exercise either, because the noise covers up the sharpening of

17

weapons, fights, and the destruction of the cell doors and walls. Weak units, weak officers, Correctional Officers, and POS's let inmates conduct these activities. Guards know why to stop inmates who try this BS, and we know how to stop it too. For instance if the Northern Hispanics in a pod insist on cadence, I may keep cadence with them using the shower doors. This too is noisy. Or, I might just cancel all yard program in that pod for the day, or in the whole unit for the day.

This isn't ever a problem if a Guard is in the control booth on a regular basis, but when doing just one shift, on overtime, or as a relief officer, a Guard has to know how to gain compliance with lawful orders. This is the source of the real work of an Officer, gaining compliance with lawful orders. Your methods must be effective and you must be capable of defending them against weakness by fellow officers and weakness by other staff and administrators.

Administrators, starting with Sargent's and going right on up to Federal Judges and Governors are the primary source of power for inmates: for them to violate the rules they know they need to prey on the weakness of administrators and on the Officers level of tolerance, it is a game of wills, and even the strongest willed Guard learns to pick their battles. But, never forget, if you give in to weak administrators and then the inmate gets hurt, it is you the Officer who goes to prison for failing in your duties, the administrator will point out the black and white rules and tisk tisk the thought of an Officer skirting them in any way.

When I first went to SHU the administrators ran the place with Memos: Memo after Memo. Officers kept huge files of them, and if you got called on the carpet for something, you just produced the memo that said you could act in the way you acted. It was stupid and it was petty, and administrative types tried to ruin people's lives over the interpretation of phrases that were violations of procedure anyway.

By law you can not change an Operating Procedure

(OP) legally with a memo, you can "clarify" an OP with a memo, but the legal authorization to change an OP is not vested in even a Warden, it requires due process and notifications. Underground regulation is epidemic in Government at every level in America, and probably every Nation-State. At that time it was well nigh religion in SHU.

Examples of weird situations where memos were produced would include such minutia as how to feed inmates. If an inmate was put on paper plate restriction, meaning that because of some bad behavior or another they could not be trusted with a hard plastic tray, maybe because they cut a piece out of a tray to make a weapon, or carved a gang sign into it, then the issue came up as to when to feed them this paper tray. Since the inmates in SHU are fed in their cells the efficient way to feed them is the way we did it when I got to SHU.

An Officer goes through the pods either counting the inmates or doing a security check. That Officer removes the locks from the cell doors combination feeding and handcuffing port. No SHU inmate is ever in the presence of anyone except their cellie without being in handcuffs, these are dangerous people. The locks were hung on the doors or on Sunday evening they were put into a wash basin with hot soapy water to clean them.

Next a cart was loaded with the hard plastic stackable trays containing either Breakfast or Dinner. At Breakfast brown paper bag Lunches into which the Officer had placed the piece of fresh fruit and the carton of milk that the inmate received with his breakfast were also placed on the cart. The upper tiers lunch/fruit/milk sacks would go into one of the plastic boxes milk cartons are delivered in.

Policy has varied over the years, but when I started one officer could feed a pod. Not all Units did it that way, since CO's are paid well they used to be trusted to work out details with their partners, the Guards routine went like this: You pushed your cart into the pod and fed the bottom tier off the cart. You put up to eight trays on one arm and picked up the plastic milk box with the other.

You climbed the stairs to the upper tier and threw/slid the milk crate to the far end of the tier. You opened a food port and handed the inmates their trays, you continued down the tier feeding trays, picked up the milk crate at the far end, and walking back toward the stairs you handed out lunch sacks, closing the food ports as you finished each cell. You did this as rapidly as possible. Most units did not have every cell occupied by two inmates, and Guards made certain any empty beds were on the upper tier. In contrast, weak administrators, CO's, Correctional Officers, and POS's let inmates dictate who celled where. When you finished in the pod you were in, and if you got back to the rotunda first you got to chose which pod you fed next, any Officer with an ounce of brains picked the pod with the fewest inmates on the upper tier, unless they were avoiding an inmate they knew was going to present special problems.

It took about 12 minutes for two officers to feed up to 96 inmates this way. If there were three officers available it took about 8 or 9, or a little longer if you had partners who lacked spacial awareness and got in each others way. Weak Correctional Officers, either physically weak or mentally weak, might take much longer, with this system the good officers were not bogged down by the inability of the poor officers to act efficiently.

As for paper trays, you just fed them when their turn came, it was a pain to balance them along with the real trays, but it wasn't impossible. But, administrators decided that the inmate complaints that paper trays held cold food were true, so they ruled that you had to feed the paper trays first. So after that an officer would have to wander all over the place feeding paper trays, then try to remember where they had been served, before doing the regular feeding. It was a major increase of workload for the officers. Officers simply stopped doing the paperwork to discipline inmates because of the administrators weak attitude, and if an Officer did do the paper work, often the POS officers would just give the

20

inmate a regular tray anyway to save themselves the extra work.

The trays were recovered using similar process, and trash was also collected twice a day during tray pickup. The lessened load at dinner time, just a tray to serve and no lunch sack was offset by inmates naturally throwing away more trash in the evening.

Often, however, an Officer does much much more work than this. SHU inmates are the most difficult bastards to deal with on this planet. Often they attack the officers feeding them, or they refuse to return to their cells when they have been let out for exercise yards, out for medical attention, out for a talk about issues with people from the appeals office, or out for any of dozens of other events that they were released for.

Then there would be a team of Officers organized to deal with the crisis. You can not let an inmate take a part of the prison hostage. When they do other inmates can not receive medical care, either on an ongoing basis or in an emergency. If you let them hold the area hostage another inmate will manipulate the situation to say they need urgent care, if we fail to supply it, the inmate has a court case that is winnable. In many cases the inmate who created the crisis is in cahoots with the inmate needing medical care. To them life is a game of chance, they roll the dice hoping that the system can be held financially liable to them.

When a team, called an Extraction Team, is organized the work of the prison they were scheduled to do is canceled or done by the remaining officers. In my early days in SHU, on Third watch from 14:00 to 22:00 hours, there was almost a non stop crisis.

To drive a wedge between one group of Officers and another, inmates would act up without enough time left on Second Watch for the crisis to be resolved. Oncoming officers in the Third Watch group perpetually felt like Second Watch had left the mess for Third Watch to clean up. In many cases it was true too. Some POS officers would even instigate conflicts that they knew they could walk away from.

On one shift I fed either alone or with one other officer seven housing units, and picked up the trays in a dozen. In one night I have done five extractions of inmates, and the team I was on was not the only one. Those night were in no way a record number. Other Officers have worked just as hard or harder on a regular basis.

Officers were in charge of mail too. You learned to process mail as the very first thing when you came on duty and do it fast. It was not a question of would an alarm go off but when. Remember all of us reported to every alarm.

You got the mail done partly to mollify the inmates. If you did not have it done by the time you fed them the inmates would berate you, and if it was not done by the time you picked up trays then some of those sons of bitches would keep their trays, creating more emergencies. It seemed so normal at the time, a challenge, and an opportunity to develop skills and techniques to keep your area of responsibility functioning, to keep it under control, to keep it safe.

And these emergencies were not just petty things. If you have never thought about what it looks like to watch a human being kick in the skull of another human being, let me tell you how it goes.

We had just left a meeting, there were always meetings to tell us that it was dangerous and we needed to be safe – duh motherfuckers. So anyway at the meeting we were told that under no circumstances were we to open a cell door exposing inmates to staff unless the inmates were handcuffed. This was the policy and we knew it and lived it religiously, but some one felt like wasting our time telling us. Just minutes later, back in our unit we heard the noise of a cell fight. Two inmates who lived together were fighting in their cell. We responded into C Section, Tom Blower was in front of me, and on the upper tier one inmate, wearing hard shoes, was kicking in his cellies head, blood was everywhere. We yelled for him to stop, but he did not.

Now the danger is that this is being faked, and if you open the door both inmates will attack with shanks, heavy metal swords they have produced themselves. Or maybe a stolen screwdriver, or lost Leather-man Tool.

But this day there was no mistaking the fact that the inmate on the floor being kicked would be lucky to live, and would not walk out of that cell. So we had the Control Booth Officer open the door. By that time there were 10 or a 12 of us on the upper tier. The kicking inmate knew we would come after him with our PR-24 Side Handle Batons, this was before Pepper Spray was a part of our tool kit, though a Sargent would have had a Mace canister, but there were no Sargent's here yet.

The assailant said he would cuff up, so with the door cracked an inch or so, but definitely open, we cuffed him and got the door open all the way. The nearly dead cellie was also cuffed up before he was moved. We had saved his life, and we were absolutely certain we were in trouble. We had violated a very sacred policy and we had made the decision to do it minutes after signing our names to a record of having been told not to do it. I probably had six or seven years service at that time and Officer Blower had about the same. In addition a dozen other Officers had been with us.

But like I say there is policy and then there is policy. Even though we did what we always did and told on ourselves, we were forgiven without a word said. If it had gone bad, if the assailant had come through that door and hurt Officers we would have all faced up to and including time in prison, instead without a word of thanks the administrators simply never mentioned the incidents particulars. But, you never knew if your judgment would be accepted or if you would be prosecuted.

Double Life

Today, at Home Depot and Wal-Mart and Fisherman's Restaurant, I saw dozens of people I worked with at PBSP over the years. I added two former PBSP Officers to my Face Book friends. There were at least one I used to hate on Face Book, Mark Highland was the other one, kind of funny after writing about him yesterday. He is going to retire the day he turns 50. We can retire at 50 because the job is so stress filled. In America right now that is viewed as a terrible injustice. But even though I love the Conservatives, most of them couldn't make it a full hour in SHU, much less survive a career. And, lots of us retire early from injuries. Injuries from inmates, injuries from other staff while trying to subdue inmates, injuries from the sheer effort of feeding the lazy scum. Retirement is the uppermost thing on an Officers mind.

I retired twice.

The other Face Book person today was Dave Barcycle. I used to hate him. When I started to try to write this about 3 months ago, it was unreadable. Like I tell my son, all I could put down on paper is I hate that fucking place. Let me tell you why I hated Dave, and why I don't hate him anymore.

PBSP is a popular place with documentary film makers.

My children have seen me in a documentary, but I don't know which one. I almost never watch them. National Geographic made one that I really like. I got to watch my cousin Reggie Loftin and his brother in law in that one, responding on B-yard, the site of PBSP's biggest riots. And, it showed one of the most disgusting inmates, make that most disgusting humans, there is, Ivory "Double Life" Taylor. Taylor looks up at the camera and says, "They sprayed me with a fire extinguisher." A true statement.

"Double Life" is a black man, and an officially

designated Management Problem. He is a seriously twisted and disgusting person. He smears his penis with butter and presses it onto paper creating what he calls a "Shillong O Gram", he tries to give them to female officers and staff, he tries to have them photocopied at the SHU Law Library. All inmate photocopies are done by Law library Staff. He mails them to Female and Male federal Judges. Federal judges do not like to receive Shillong O Gram's.

When the National Geographic was filming they had a reporter standing in front of the infamous "Double Life" Taylor in his cell. They had to stop because, as my Land and Cattle partner, and retired Guard Tom King likes to tell it, "He was sucking his own dick". Tom was there, He said the cameraman looked up from the camera, over the reporters shoulder and said, "Oh hell no!", the activity did not make it into the National Geographic show.

Taylor hurt many Officers over the years, he would smear his body with baby oil, why the hell inmates can buy baby oil is a subject for later, and so a team trying to extract him had a hard time actually getting a hold of him. In his early days he was very strong, later he pulled some incredibly long hunger strikes, over 40 days during the time period I am about to describe, and lost some of his ability to fight. By then we had Pepper Spray anyway, and having your skin on fire is not as satisfying to inmates as dislocating an officers shoulder or knee.

I had Taylor as one of the inmates in my units, or units that I had responsibilities in, many times over the years. But the last time was the most challenging time.

I injured my feet at PBSP, and for years and years I suffered great pain. When it happened I was, as often happens, in the best shape of my life. I was a dedicated gym rat, could do leg presses at an incline of over 800 pounds and calf raises on a machine of almost he same amount. Far from being muscle bound, I used the Table for the 1.5 Mile Run Test in the NAHC's 1986 book All About Elk as my guide, and could do the run in an "Excellent" 10 to 11 minutes. My children and I swam once a week, and we also went to a weekly boxing clinic where we spent an hour doing boxing work outs for 3 minutes at a time with a one minute rest period. I could skip rope, including backwards criss crosses for up to an hour at a time. The injury happened as fate would have it, not at the hands of an inmate, but instead was caused by a food cart. PBSP's food carts had at that time a really goofy latch. Officers closed the latches by kicking them.

I was in a hurry. Officers can do shift swaps. I can work someone else's shift in exchange for them working my shift. It is a great benefit for those that wish to use it. Just before I was injured I worked a Relief Position – I filled in for Officers who worked five days a week by doing their job on their Regular Days Off (RDO's). On my Monday and Tuesday I was a control booth officer, then for two days I was the floor officer, then for the last day I was the control booth officer in the unit where I worked on the floor. I was working in C-Shu's first corridor units C-1 through C-6. My two units were C-2 and C-3.

Before I took this position C-1 had been designated as PBSP's "Violence Control Unit" or VCU. It was a cesspool. By this time the name had been changed to Management Control Unit, but it was never called MCU. I don't know why, probably because it was just a memo change and thus not designated in the Operations Procedure Manual #222 – SHU Operations (OP 222), the Operations Procedure manual for SHU.

Anyway I was dedicated to becoming an Elk hunter, and in really good shape, I did over 100 shift swaps a year, all with officers in the first corridor, and never in C-1. One day a Captain asked me if I was "the regular", meaning the officer assigned to a unit five days a week to a unit, and I told him, "In this Corridor I am the regular everywhere." Most people agreed.

I took my 100 swaps off to spend time with my children, even though I was divorced I spent a great deal of time with them. We did livestock programs with the 4-H and Grange. I also hiked some, and I hunted the West backpacking for Elk, Deer, and Bear. I had the world by the tail.

This cart fucked me up. I kicked the latch and pain shot through my leg like the bone was broken. I have been told since then that the foot has a loop of nerves, the only place in the human body like it, where there are two nodules of nerve endings. I had injured that part of my body.

Soon I had to change my job, which was not difficult, officers bid for the positions they want based on seniority. I went back to control booths, I couldn't go to the gym, at about the same time, and without me knowing it, my gall bladder went bad. I was always in pain, miserable. It was not something I was prepared for. While I had had weight gain in my early twenties, for most of my life I had been a strong man, I grew up on a Ranch and was in my element working hard. I compensated for my condition and thought it would heal. And, to some degree I continued to work hard, doing overtimes and swaps and I started using more and more sick leave.

Sick leave is one of the State of California's most schizophrenic "benefits". They give you tons of it, and call you vile and loathsome for using it, or for saving it up and cashing it in at retirement. Your dammed if you do and dammed if you don't, which is nothing unusual for an Officer, but if you use it your supervisors treat you like low life maggot scum.

At some point, maybe three years after hurting my feet, and even though I had been under doctors care for it, it was just getting worse. I had stopped doing swaps and overtime, and I finally had the seniority to get a second watch job in SHU. I took the floor officer position in C-6. It had the shortest walk to the kitchen, so I only had to push the food carts a short distance, and I decided if I couldn't do this position I would have to face the fact I couldn't be an officer. The incident responding to Roast's attack had recently

27

happened, and the running on that day had left me in
constant pain. The one big drawback was that "Double Life"
Taylor was housed in A-section Cell 101, and Dave Barcycle
was the acting Captain of C-SHU. At the time I did not think
it meant anything, but it did.

In violation of policy the SHU Law Library had
simply stopped making photocopies for I/M Taylor. The
Officers in the law library could get no help from their
supervisors in their efforts to stop the photocopying of his
penis. I/M Taylor claimed to the Federal Courts that his
rights were being violated when CDC disciplined him for
masturbating in front of staff. His claim is that his religion,
"the Religion of Rosco" involved worshiping "Rosco" , his
penis. Jerking and sucking himself off was how I/M Taylor
"worships Rosco". I/M Taylor sent the photocopies of
Roscoe in his legal paperwork to Federal Judges. The Judges
ordered CDC to stop sending them photocopies, and in some
cases the paper and butter originals too.

Managers being worthless, they ordered the officers
to stop I/M Taylor, but did not say how. When I got to the
new job Taylor thought that he was entitled to have the floor
officer make photo copies for him. As a Guard I was
unwilling to follow this POS policy.

I stopped doing it and I/M Taylor went on a rampage.
To calm him down Acting Captain (Captain (A)) Barcycle
did something spectacularly stupid.

One of the tasks that needs to be done is the cleaning
of the prison. Why they don't just hire janitors is a monument
to the pure ignorance that underlies "Progressive" and liberal
theology. Why shouldn't the inmates be used to clean the
prison they say, and then they make it public policy. It is a
stupid, stupid idea. Inmates that are assigned or volunteer to
clean are called porters. Porter positions are coveted because
of the ability porters have to pass messages, weapons, drugs,
and other contraband. If the wrong inmate has the position he
will be stabbed by the gangsters in order to get some other,
more acceptable inmate, into the position. In SHU, porter is a

28

voluntary position. Inmates with the classification to be in SHU are by law not allowed to hold a job in prison. If an inmate has a job while in prison his point score declines faster than if he does his time without an assignment, jobs are one kind of assignment, education is another. Inmates want out go to school and work not for the reasons you and I do, but instead they want their sentences shortened and they want to live in a lower custody level setting.

So anyway, after Taylor goes on a rampage, on my RDO's, Captain Barcycle tells Taylor he can have the C-6 "A" Section volunteer porter job. Porters work on third watch, it just doesn't work out for them to be out in the section at other times. Second watch runs inmates to and from the units so they can go to the dentist, see doctors, go to the law library, go out to court, to go to educational testing, and who knows what else, o yes and to go rat on one another. Third watch said no way.

Third Watch's Lieutenant told Captain Barcycle that he would not require his Officers to deal with an idiot like Taylor being the porter. So Dave decides we will have Taylor work on Second Watch. So my control booth Officer Joey Lesina and I take a deep breath and say we will give it a try. And, at first, we make it work. But, underlying all this is Taylors drive to manipulate the situation.

During this time all the legal work that was not photo copied is found in a drawer in the law library. Taylor is amazed at his luck, if they had been thrown away as they arrived in the law library mail it would have been bad enough, but now there is proof, and Taylor thinks his luck has changed for the best. Because despite the nick name "Double Life", I/M Taylor is close to his release date. And, he pictures winning millions in a lawsuit. His rights have been violated. Both his right to access the legal system and his right to practice his religion.

He has a hearing coming up on these issues. It will be heard by a Lieutenant. In preparation Taylor starts trying to implant the idea in my head that I knew about some aspect of

29

the situation, I was frankly curious about the reason for him trying to manipulate me, so I went along.

Now like I said at first it worked. Taylor cleaned and he went back to his cell when asked. On my last day of work before Christmas, I was about to empty the unit's coffee pot, but I held it up to the control booth and asked Lesina if he wanted any before I tossed it. He said no. Then I saw Taylor, face pressed up to the perforated steel of a Section wall. I asked him how long it had been since he had a cup of real coffee, he said it had been over ten years. Now, of course to give him a cup was a policy violation, but Guards don't care, but I care about my partners. So Lesina and I agree that to reward our legendary asshole porter for a job done well he could have a cup of coffee. He took it and went "back to his house". Prison slang for returned to his cell.

Now Taylor is a manipulator, a pervert, violent, and weird looking too, but is also, to some degree pretty funny. Even the time he was sprayed with a fire extinguisher was in character for him. He is naturally skinny, and could almost escape through a food or handcuff port, and for years anyone not paying attention to him would find him half in and half out of a cell or holding cage if they left the port unlocked. One day he jumped up to the windows of the second floor control booth and tried to squeeze into the booth, where there is a control Booth Officer and at that time two rifles and a pistol. It is the general consensus of everyone who knows Taylor that the Officer should have watched him climb into the booth and then should have shot him dead. That would have been within policy, but there are policies and then there are policies, so the officer picks up the fire extinguisher and uses it to force Taylor off the ledge and back onto the floor. The officer is disciplined for using inappropriate force. Policy was eventually changed to allow for "Unconventional" force, because it was so obvious that this wasn't really a bad solution. Of course Pepper Spray is the tool available now for resolving this issue.

The day after Christmas, when Taylor comes out to

30

work he comes over to talk to me. "Hey Mac, about that coffee." he says. I say, "Hold on, that was a one time deal, your not holding it over my head and your not getting a cup on a regular basis." "No, no, no, Mac, Do you know what its like to have your first big old cup of coffee and then go back into a little cell? I went crazy in there, this Nigger don't want no more coffee." Taylor always referred to himself as either "A nigger" or "This nigger". When I tell this story anyone who ever knew Taylor cracks up, it is typical of him.

But his reaction to the hearing with the Lt. was typical too. When he tried to get me to regurgitate the scenario he had tried to plant in my head I stopped him and told the Lt. that I was wondering why he had tried to get me to say whatever it was, but now it was obvious. Taylor went ballistic, and remains furious at me to this day.

The result of an investigation into his violated legal rights resulted in Dave Barcycle never making Captain, and a whole group of Lt's and Sgt.'s getting disciplined. I suspect some of them lost pay for a while. I talked to an investigator and pretty much stood up to them trying to scape goat me for the fiasco. But, I don't suffer foolishness lightly and because I had done my job I wasn't in trouble.

I also was not at work. My feet were so bad I spent almost 4 months unable to walk, I had developed Deep Vein Thrombosis from putting my feet up to stop the pain. In the last months before I went out injured I actually would soak my feet in ice water after feeding inmates. In all I was off work for two years, 10 months of them I was retired. But eventually I got healed, and went back to SHU. For a while some of the supervisors still hated me. Hated me for having gone out on disability, for having had a history of sick leave "abuse", though I never did use up all my leave, or receive any disciplinary action, either formal or informal, for being sick so much, and they hate me for protecting myself from being the fall guy for their mismanagement. There are always managers who fuck up, and they are always trying to blame someone else. I am still extra sensitive to this

31

American way of doing business. It is a culture deeply ingrained into management in general, and CDC(R) in particular.

Mike Couthperson called today and I talked to him about writing about prison. I have known Mike since we were teenagers. He said he tried to write about working in prison, but hated thinking about the place. I understand. I find it difficult to regurgitate the bile of my experiences too.

Since writing about Dave Barcycle I friended him on Facebook, or sent an invite, now that I think about it I am not sure he accepted.

As I go about my business in Crescent City, CA and our neighboring community of Brookings, OR I often see people I know from work. More often now I find myself better able to enjoy seeing them.

There is no one way to handle the duties and challenges of working in prison. When you want to proceed in a given way, the one that works for you in the circumstance of the moment, and an inmate refuses to go along with the program you have to ask others to help you. Sometimes no one around at the time will see it your way. Later, after the fact others will Monday morning the situation and wonder why you did not fight to do it the way you desired.

C-11

The position that shaped me as a Guard and taught me the most was being the Control Booth Officer in SHU unit C-11 on third watch. My main duties in Charlie 11 Control were to control inmate movement and facilitate safe Officer access to inmates and the physical spaces in C-11. I provided gun coverage while inmates accessed exercise yard, exchanged their laundry, came and went from medical, legal, disciplinary, educational, and other services. And while Officers delivered mail, canteen, annual packages, meals, and other services, and while they inspected and searched common areas and cells for damage, contraband, and evidence.

My 1997 Time book shows an entry on May 12th, "Garza Gone" and a smiley face with a notation "9 mo 9 days of Garza", so I must have taken over C-11 Control in August of 1996. I/M Garza CDC Number D-00596, a White inmate, is the only inmate of whom I know their CDC Number by heart. Almost 15 years later I still remember it. I/M Garza acted the fool every hour of every day, and would constantly yell, "I am inmate Garza D-00596 and I take full responsibility for my actions." Which was a lie, he always denied responsibility for what he did. The motivation for him being a constant violator of the rules was because he is a weak frail man and feared contact with other inmates. He is in prison because as a 19 year old he walked into a park and stabbed a 17 year old boy who was talking to a girl who had rejected Garza after one or two dates.

The first program ran on third watch was showers. When I went to work in SHU there was a terrible management practice of issuing memos everyday based on the crisis of the moment. By law the OP 222 should define the programs to be ran, when to run them, and the standard way to run them. But, instead CDC at that time ran on memo after memo after memo. As I mentioned before, Officers had

33

huge binders full of memos,and if anyone challenged the way they managed things during their shift they would pull out their favorite memo and say that here was the proof that they were doing it right. There were too many memos being generated to allow for formal training, and when the managers tried to hold training meetings savvy Officers would point out that the memo in question was contrary to OP 222 and thus unenforceable. This angered the petty tyrants in management and they would conduct personal vendettas against Officers.

A good example was Lt. J Ridle, who would call meetings on Second Watch to complain that the Officers were stupid and lazy because they had not finished feeding yet. Officers would go back to their units, sit down and wait hours to pick up trays and trash. As a new Officer I asked once why we were not getting it done, and getting on to other programs like medical and yard: and of course the Guard said to me, "You heard Lt. Ridle, I am too stupid and too lazy to get feeding done on time."

Looking at the OP 222 as a new Control Booth Officer I determined to run my shower program by the book. Eight minutes of shower time, beginning when I opened the cell door for the inmates to go to the shower, a two minute warning, and it was time for the inmates to go home. I started at 14:00 and expected to shower four cells per pod, either the upper tier or the lower tier on alternating days, by 15:00 hours. Inmates don't like being rushed, they don't like following the rules, and they do love to challenge an Officer's will to do things the way the Officer wants them done.

For the first few months it was like pulling teeth. But I was dedicated to enforcing my will, and I had tools at my disposal. The greatest power a Control Booth Officer had was the canceling of program. Yards were one program that inmates love. It is one of their chances to communicate to other inmates outside of their pod and unit, and they like the change of scenery, and the exercise. It is impossible to really

34

take away showers. An inmate is entitled to a shower every 72 hours, almost: actually he is entitled to access to a shower every 72 hours. If he refuses, that is on him. I considered it a refusal if you stopped to talk at the cell front of another inmate, which all by itself is a violation of OP 222. So wise inmates would stop in front of other cells on their way back from the shower to their cells. The inmates going to shower would have already had their yard for the day, so you could not take away their yard that day, and if you wanted to say an inmate refused yard it had to be in the moment. For example if they were on their way to yard and stopped to talk you could close the yard door, open their cell door and tell them to return to their house because stopping to talk constituted a refusal of yard, same thing on the way to showers.

So what to do if they didn't go home from their showers. If multiple inmates in a pod did it on an ongoing basis, or on a given afternoon, you could cancel yard. You just logged them all as refusing. But, they might react by holding all their food trays, and thereby creating a crisis. When a Sargent responded to solve the crisis, the inmates would complain about your action. The supervisor would tell you to write up the ones causing trouble and not punish the others. Of course then I would take hours writing the inmate up, and in the meantime I would suspend the whole units yards because I was writing.

This kind of ongoing confrontation was stressful in the extreme. And, inmates would go far beyond simply stopping in front of a cell. In those days you never knew how a SHU inmate was going to behave when you let them out of a cell. They might charge at your control booth and throw a milk carton full of piss and shit at you. They might do it to another inmates cell. They might throw it at the floor officers station. Or they could take the pod hostage, demanding to see supervisors for some perceived injustice. And it was not only over their issues with the on duty staff. They were mad over medical issues, legal issues, visiting issues, canteen

35

issues, disciplinary issues, in fact any thing that happened in prison might be used as an excuse to start a disruption. It was thought by many inmates, and their lawyers, that if SHU could be kept disrupted enough that eventually the courts would blame the SHU itself and release them from that confinement.

Inmates would try to steal razors during showers, or just take the blade out of a disposable razor, replacing it perhaps with a thin strip of foil.

One evening I/M Garza went to shower under escort, and after all yards were completed in his pod, but before chow. When it was time to escort him home he refused to return the razor, saying he never received one. He soaped himself up again and started to sing, from the Control booth I turned off the water leaving him covered in soap. Policy at the time was such I simply called my Sargent, told him the situation, and asked him not to come into the unit that evening. We explained to Garza that he would not be fed unless he was in his cell, and so his actions constituted a refusal of his evening meal. At the 21:00 hours count Garza gave the razor back to the Officer doing count and asked to go home. We pointed out the fact that it was a violation of policy to move inmates in SHU after 20:30 hours and thanked him for returning the razor. We spoke to the First Watch Sargent, and he talked to the Watch Commander and it was decided that Garza would remain in the shower until Second Watch. As luck would have it I was scheduled to be the Second Watch Control Officer. When I came in Garza was in the shower, he did not know at first who was in Control, and was very disappointed to find out it was me.

The Second Watch Officers fed and picked up that pod before 07:00, the time when inmate movement was started. They did not leave his lunch sack in the cell, and told Garza if he went home at 07:00, without problems, he would receive his lunch, even though policy was for him not to receive it because he was not in his cell during feeding by his own choice. Garza went home, and was upset when told he

36

would receive his lunch at lunch time. But, not too upset because he knew I would be there all day including his next dinner time.

So foil was banned in SHU, but then some medicines came in foil, so if they couldn't get the foil and the med, they filed suite. For many years the medical staff would put medicines in the control booth and it was expected that Officers would disperse the meds when the inmate asked for them. If you complained that the inmates were just using this as an excuse to get out of their cells to talk and pass contraband you were told to have your floor staff walk the med into the pod to the inmates cell. Years later I filed on this, and would call the medical staff to come down to the unit to hand out meds because Officers were not medically licensed. This actually brought an end to the practice.

I could write all day about I/M Garza and his bizarre misbehavior – but one story makes an important point. I/M Garza always did petty violations, he was a cell warrior. At one time in C-11 we wrote up every single violation he committed, it was a lot of extra work, but he stopped being a constant pain right after the shower incident. And, in a few months there came a night when he was not on any restrictions due to his behavior. He even went to his shower and back and forth to yard without causing a disruption. After chow that evening all the yards were finished early. Around 19:30 it was quiet and peaceful. The devil entered me for a moment. I reached over and started opening the lower tier shower door in F-Pod. Then I started opening I/M Garza's upper tier cell door. Now over the years the only people who had grown to hate I/M Garza more than the Officers were the other inmates. They had gotten good and tired of the program being suspended in their pod and the unit and all of SHU due to Garza's passive aggressive nonsense. As soon as Garza heard two doors opening, one being his he started screaming, "Hey Mac, Hey C/O, close this door, close this door, ..." He was terrified that he would have to fight another inmate. I closed his door and the shower door, and he started cussing me like no ones business. The inmates in his pod started laughing their asses off, they yelled to the other pods what I had done and the whole place was crazy with laughter at cell warrior Garza's expense. With a shit eating grin on my face I looked down from the Control Booth at the Officers station and told them what I had done, Guard Pebles and Guard Kiler busted a gut too. Later they asked me how I had thought of doing that, "Fuck that guy" is my response.

Of course there were some "good" inmates. Inmates who never caused trouble, and there were bad inmates, ones who always caused trouble. But many of them were in between, some only acting out when a "good inmate" who was his superior in the gang structure, would have them act up, thus using surrogates to cause trouble while retaining the veneer of being a "good inmate". Knowing all the politics of prison a Guard learned to make sure the pain of lost programs was liberally distributed. If I was going to cancel yard I would never mention it until after tray and trash pickup.

To make sure I had control I exercised my right to keep the number of programs going on at any one time to a minimum. For instance a Correctional Officer would be bullied into running one cell to yard before starting showers, and even changing out yards during showers. I would not run a yard until showers were over, similarly I did not start yards in between chow being served and the trays being recovered. It is amazing how much faster showering goes when some "big homie" gang boss was wanting to get his yard before dinner was served. For the most part an inmate was entitled to an hour and one half of yard each day. But, there really isn't time to run a full pod of eight cells for 1.5 hours every day. It would mean yard was available for 12 hours of the day. But yard doesn't open until 07:00 and must be finished by 20:30 or so, about 13hours 30 minutes. But yards have to be closed from 13:30 until third watch is ready to start them again. Close for showers and for dinner, and maybe lose time

38

if breakfast was not served until after 7:00 and you are pressed for time.

When alarms sounded in SHU you lost your floor staff, they ran to the alarm(s), this could delay handing out razors during showers. Now some Correctional Officers would hand out razors from control booths, but this was a violation of OP 222, and as I/M Taylor's fire extinguisher incident points out this policy was in effect for good reason. An inmate could get your arm and possible kill you either with a weapon of his own, or by his bare hands, and if you had your pistol on your hip, or your rifle slung over your shoulder they might get a gun too. I did it in my early days, but not much. Later I stopped completely. I had a strong enough will that I could tell the inmates no, you will have to wait.

But of course you have to look for opportunities to build rapport, if only for your own sanity, because inmates did run officers off from their positions just from the sheer weight of their aggressive tactics and strategies, devised to allow them to run the unit the way they desired. One of the biggest frustrations of being an Officer is the situation where you go into a unit for an overtime or a swap and they try to game you when you have years and years of service.

All of PBSP went on lock down a few months after I started in C-11. By then the unit knew I was a certified asshole who would make the whole unit miserable if given any reason. My floor staff was Jason Pebles as Search and Escort Officer (S&E) and Brian Kiler as Floor Officer (Floor) four days a week and Rick Kastor as floor one day a week. They enjoyed having a strong Control because it stopped a lot of the inmates from bothering them. The lock down was done so that the entire prison could be searched, and it took weeks to search the whole prison. Each night all the Floor and S&E's would go to a unit, empty a pod of inmates, and search every cell and all the showers yards and common spaces.

About two weeks into the searching I came on duty

on my Monday, my days off were during what most people think of as the workweek, I think Wednesdays and Thursdays (not bad because I have Thanksgiving off – LOL) but I had been gone for three days that weekend. Brian and Jason left as soon as I gave them their equipment. Soon inmates began calling out and asking me about getting showers, one of the "good" inmates told me that they had not had showers since my Thursday, or about 96 hours ago. Just because we are on lock down it does not mean that the 72 hour rule is forgotten. During lock down officers are often required to take every inmate from his cell to shower in handcuffs and escorted by two officers, all escorts in SHU are conducted by two officers for one inmate and three officers for two inmates, and most of the cells had two inmates. It makes for a slow process sharing officers with the unit across the hall to be in compliance with CDC's rules.

I looked in the units logbook and the days I was gone all showed lock down no showers. I called other units and the other officers verified that there had been no shower during those three days. The last call I made was to my Sargent, he basically said they had no plan to do showers that day.

I don't play that game, I have no desire to explain to a Federal jury why I aided in cruel and unusual punishment, and that is what skipping showers for that long amounted to. I thought for a few moments, and looking back I have always been amazed at my solution.

I opened the door to the first cell in A-pod. A black inmate stepped out. I told him that it was wrong for them to not have showers. I told him loudly that I knew they hated me, and this was their chance to fuck me, and they knew it too, I was outside of policy and vulnerable. But, I was going to shower the whole unit, they would not get razors, and if anyone took more than ten minutes, held up the program, or did anything except go to and from the shower, then I was shutting it down for the rest of them. By 15:30 all eight cells in each of the six pods had had a shower. I even let inmate

Garza and any others on "escort status" go on their own. I even got a few "thank you"s. And, I logged it. I logged anything out of ordinary during my whole career. I wanted to be able to show any investigator when and why I provided services or denied them.

When Brian and Jason came back to the unit to feed chow they said they were going to take their time because they were tired from searching and they had been told to shower the unit after chow. I cemented their friendship for life when I told them the unit was already showered. They traded off going to the unit next door for double celled escorts, and laughed a lot.

That moment made C-11 my unit. The inmates knew I was tough but fair, and that I cared somewhat about them as human beings. Somewhat. It was also a Guard like deed. One to be talked about.

The Day to Day

Officer love to talk. It is a way to relieve the stress of dealing with ignorance and obstinacy from supervisors, staff, fellow officers and inmates. All of whom could be difficult at any given time. Some of the time because they wanted to overlook rules and other times because they wanted to be overly tied to them. Showering those inmates was a direct violation of the rules. It was also under the circumstances the right thing to do. That Sargent should have known that PBSP was not going to overlook showering those inmates that day, in fact he should have been grateful for those of us who called him that afternoon and gave him a heads up on the situation. There are times when Guards let supervisors fail.

One evening I was on an extraction team. We were actually doing an insertion, returning I/M Scavinski Hymes, a black man, to his cell after he had held a holding cell hostage by refusing to submit to handcuffs for a few hours.

Hymes is a legendary POS inmate. He fought daily at times. I first met him working with Mike Couthperson on Third Watch as a Floor Officer. While we were feeding Hymes tried to grab at me through the feeding/cuff port. I jerked my knee up and almost slammed the port door on Hymes hand.

I was very new to PBSP at the time, and was surprised when Mike told me Hymes would file a complaint on me because it was a policy violation to force the port closed if the inmate was "holding the port" hostage. So, I walked down to the Sergeants Office and told on myself. The astonished Sargent just said thanks for letting him know.

We went back into the pods to pick up the trays, and I stopped in front of Hymes cell. I asked him if he was going to return his tray. He said sure because, "I am going to spend my evening writing you up McNamara." Inmates have a complaint form CDC(r)-602, an idea from The Rand Corporation,the same think tank that gave us the Vietnam era managerial fiasco. I took the tray and told him I had already told on myself. He looked puzzled. I told him I didn't know the policy, but Couthperson had told me I was wrong, and if he wrote a complaint he could include in it my admission to the Sargent. He never did a complaint, or "602 me", and despite being a true master at violence and disruption, Hymes rarely caused me trouble.

One time when he did, he broke a sprinkler head in his cell. He was so used to acting out that he had forgotten the fact he had just gotten a TV. When I ran into the pod to see what he had done, he was hunched over the TV trying to keep the water off of it. I went to turn off the sprinkler, and took so much time at it, almost half an hour, that a Lt. chewed me out big time for it. But, Hymes laughed about it, "You had me Mac."

Another day Hymes was in a holding cell and saw me eating a hamburger, I asked him how long it had been since he had a real hamburger, he said he had fast food ones now and then when he was being escorted to Southern California for court dates, but couldn't remember when he had a real one. It reminded me that I had heard that he had told other Officers that when he paroled he was going to open a Bar-B-Que place in Crescent City, I asked him and he said it was true that that was his plan. I said to him, "Hell Hymes, we have bar-b-Que in my backyard, if you end up living here your welcome to come over." He looked at me, and the two other officers standing there who honestly wondered what the hell I was doing, and a look of understanding came over Hymes face: "Fuck that" he said.

The night of the insertion Hymes had been placed in a holding cell to cut his toe nails. A pair of toe nail clippers can be used as a weapon, or used to cut the soft steel in a cell to produce weapon stock, they can be used to strip electrical cords which can be wired to a steel door to shock an Officer, While clippers were always to be watched closely, it was even more important to watch them when inmates like Hymes, or Taylor, or Garza, had control of them.

43

So Hymes returned the clippers, which become a weapon as soon as he possesses them without authorization for their use as clippers, but refused to cuff up and go home. The Lt. in charge that evening was both a new Lt., and not very savvy, much less up to speed on SHU operations. When he said he was not going to use pepper spray on Hymes he said it was because, "Hymes isn't bothered by pepper spray." Those of us on the extraction team removed our gear and told the Sargent we refused to do an extraction under those circumstances.

The Sgt. convinced the Lt. that it would be a good idea to not rule out the use of pepper spray. As experienced cops we knew that Hymes ability to hold out when pepper spray was used hinged on access to water and blankets. A wet blanket over the head could lessen the effects of pepper spray. But, in the holding cell Hymes did not have water or blankets, he was in a t-shirt and boxer shorts, and boxer shorts don't provide any protection from the intense effects pepper spray has on male genitalia.

So as it turned out Hymes agreed to cuff up when we showed up in full extraction gear and carrying pepper spray. In his weird mind the fact we had to go to the trouble of getting an extraction team together, which included calling in the Administrator of the Day (AOD), a person of at least Captain rank but perhaps a warehouse manager or other administrator, even the head of Food Services could be AOD, a position used when no Captain or above was on duty. Hymes decided he had disrupted things enough and was not interested in spending the next couple of days with his balls on fire.

When I handcuffed him and the key was turned on the door he turned around and faced me, this is an aggressive action, and Hymes has a history of severely hurting Officers by kicking them while in handcuffs. My good friend Darrell Love had been Hymes last victim, to this day Darrel's back injuries are bothersome. But, I am professional, I crouch low so Hymes knows I will take him to the ground hard, with the hope his head hits both the wall behind him and the floor. We know each other and though I have only taken him to the ground once before, he knows that I am a big guy and agile, and I know my job. This is not his opportunity, he turns around and I take his arm to escort him, with another officer on his other arm "hands on". We then had him kneel down and we applied leg irons.

We lock a triangle of steel on a chain to Hymes handcuffs so he cannot pull away from us when one side of the handcuffs is removed, and take him to his cell, but he refuses to back up to the cuff-port and let us take the cuffs off. Policy does not allow pulling on the triangle or using it to do anything other than retain control of the cuffs.

Hymes has been through all this hundreds of times, he is always like this, looking for a mistake on our part hoping to hurt one of use or sue someone.

When we first started using the triangle we were warned not to hold the triangle when an inmate pulled on it. I watched one evening when Hymes leaned strongly into the triangle being held by (Anon.). when (Anon.) felt all of Hymes weight on the chain, then let it go, it was over two feet away from the cuff port where it stopped. Hymes was pitched forward by his effort with both feet planted. It looked painful as his arms cuffed behind his back checked his fat ass from falling forward.

When he refused to let us remove the cuffs we started insertion procedures. We opened the door, and I started to tie his feet together with sheets. I used clove hitches and a final overhand knot so that he would need to use his hands to untie the knots. Then I tie his arms using a clove hitch above one elbow.

There was a training film made of this procedure, and I was asked to demonstrate it because as a former able-seaman I knew the ropes and had a good reputation applying what we refer to as "soft restraints". I refused to do the film because soft restraints were not described in policy and while I was wiling to do them when I was involved to make sure

45

they were done right, I was not going to be filmed showing an unauthorized technique.

The film that was produced showed the knots being applied below the elbows, a recipe for disaster. Try it with your lover one night you will see how easy it is to unravel the sheets once you bend your elbows.

Then I wrapped the second arm above the elbow and twisted the ends together. This gives about 5 seconds while the inmate frees his hands. It takes a minute or so before he can use his legs and so this gives officers time to exit the cell and for the door to be slammed shut.

But, the new Lt. is feeling like exerting his authority. Since, the decision to use soft restraints has been made he has been saying he wants a mattress placed on the floor to keep Hymes from getting out. Now, Hymes cell has been stripped of everything because this evenings behavior warrants it. No one has ever heard of putting a mattress on the floor either. I don't want it there because I am going to be the last Officer out of the cell. So the Lt's. Idea is just ignored, but he repeats it numerous times.

With the soft restraints in place the leg irons are removed. My partner starts to unlock the handcuffs and all of a sudden the Lt. is in the cell with us asking where the mattress is. I tell my partner, finish removing the cuffs and go, so he does. I let go of the sheet on Hymes arms and I go out the door too: The look on the Lt.'s face will never leave me, the realization that he is in Hymes cell, alone, with Hymes arms coming free, topped by his fear Hymes can get moving quickly is priceless.

He forgets the mattress and comes out of the cell backpedaling in a big hurry. The door is slammed and as I leave I hear him still muttering about a mattress. I want to say right now I have a lot of respect for those of you on that extraction team who knew why I did not want to do a low hurdle over a mattress while exiting a cell. And, I have a lot of respect for the Sgt. that night who did the right things when his supervisor was hell bent on fucking up.

One other insertion stands out in my mind, it involved I/M Ferrez. A white inmate who was returned to custody, I/M Ferrez told the staff that received him into SHU that he was not going to stop until he costs the state a half-million dollars. And, he kept his word. In one month he took Officer Darby's whistle away from him four times. It was kind of funny listening to him blow that whistle for hour after hour until we would get it back from him.

On the day of the insertion we all noticed as we came onto our shift that Ferrez was in a holding or contraband cell near the C-SHU Corridor Control room. He was yelling and making a spectacle of himself. As soon as we got to our units we received a call for the extraction team to come up to Corridor Control, the usual assembly area. I was on the team this day and assigned to leg irons. Teams entered with a Shield man in front, followed in order by an Officer with a Short Baton who protected the shield and shield man, an Officer with handcuffs, an Officer with leg irons, and then a fifth back up Officer. All extraction teams were filmed by a camera officer, and supervised by a Sargent, a Lieutenant, and a Captain and/or an AOD. A scribe also kept a written record of the action. Some of the time the action could get complex.

We were told we would remove Ferrez from the cell and take him to his pod where he would be put into a shower, stripped, and showered, then placed in his cell. For some reason he was cooperative until we went to put him into his cell. I was escorting him hands on because he was wearing my leg irons, and the other hands on officer was big George Xner because he was the handcuff Officer, and Ferrez was wearing his handcuffs.

When we got to the cell door I/M Ferrez lifted his legs off the floor. Ferrez weighed about 160 pounds. I was about 220 in those days and George was about 4 inches taller than me and was about 260. We held him up keeping our hands-on grip. I told the people behind me that he had lifted his legs and the AOD said, "Put him on the floor.".

47

George and I were both veterans of hundreds of extractions or other situations where inmate's actions dictated the use of physical force. We landed on I/M Ferrez hard enough to stun him. We laid there about a minute, and I asked again, what do you want us to do? "Stand him up and try again."

Ferrez was stood up and again he lifted his legs. We asked what to do, and got the same answer. This scene was repeated for a total of four hard landings – on camera. At this point I said to George, "I don't know about you, but I have had enough camera time doing this." "No shit" he said.

We yelled for them to bring us sheets and to strip his cell. It took about five minutes and I had Ferrez trussed up in soft restraints. George held the sheets at his arms and I removed the leg irons and the handcuffs. George said to me "Hold on a second." and let go of the sheets.

"Hey Ferrez, your free, if you want to fight. Mac is going to leave and I am going to get up really slowly, how about it." he whispered.

I got up and walked out. George came out about 30 seconds later, Ferrez had not moved.

As soon as the door was closed he started kicking it and screaming his lungs out. He laid around pretending he could not get out of the sheets for almost an entire day. But, he never twitched an eyebrow for the minutes he was free to attack us.

Ferrez, Taylor, Hymes and Garza constantly disrupted the program in their area. Each received either 128's or 115's – disciplinary actions named for the State Document Number that were used to write up the charges against them, hundreds or thousands of times. Day after day they were unconcerned about the consequences. The reason is that in CA an inmate is given a certain length of sentence, say 10 years. If he behaves, works or participates in education or religious programs he can receive "day for day" meaning he gets a day off of his sentence for each day of good behavior

48

The availability of programs varies with the Level of Incarceration. The level is determined using a wide variety of factors that are evaluated when the inmate comes into the system, and is re-evaluated at least once a year, and anytime an inmate is transferred, and every 3 months if the inmate is confined in SHU.

Some of the factors are, the crime, the length of sentence, prior incarceration, family including marital status, participation in programs, and disciplinary history. The highest level of incarceration is Level IV.

SHU is not a higher level, but is earned by the inmate if he is violent, a gang participant, refuses to cell up with other inmates, or for a couple of other miscellaneous reasons. There is nowhere near enough SHU housing to hold the gang members so many of them do their SHU time in an Administrative Segregation Unit (AD SEG) or even while walking free on the Main Line.

Part of the process is the tracking of an Inmates points: The State of California's California Code of Regulations Title 15: Crime Prevention and Corrections (The Title 15, or Title 15) is the book that contains the basic rules governing inmates, staff, and management within the CA prison system. The *Updated through January 1, 2011* edition is 259 pages of 8.5 by 11 inch size, organized two columns to a page. It starts at Chapter 1. Rules and Regulations of Adult Operations and Programs, Article 1. Behavior Section 3000 Definitions, and runs to Sub-chapter (sic) 6. ADULT PAROLE Article 20. Revocation Proceedings [Reserved] Section 3815 Limitations of Parole Service.

Article 10 - Classification 3375. defines the process of classification which is conducted by Committees formed of Counselors, the Peace Officer classification for the staff that tracks and calculates an inmates incarceration factors, who are designated either Correctional Counselor I, II, or III.

CCI's earn a salary that tops out around the higher Lt. Range, and CCII's are in the range of Captains, with CCIII's working at the level comparable to an Associate Warden. Committees require three staff members one at the CCI level, a CCII, and a Captain, only two of whom can be acting out of their normal classification, for example a CCI, filling a CCII role, or a CCII as a Captain, for Unit Classification Committees or with the top position an Associate Warden (AW) or an AW Acting (AW(A)). for Institutional Classification Committees (ICC). Don't worry if this seems complicated, in actuality I am simplifying it for you, and it is a daily challenge to form committees that are lawful.

The next section of The Title 15, 3375.1 Inmate Placement (a) (1) begins by describing Level 1 inmates as those with 0 to 18 points. These inmates are housed in dormitories or converted gymnasiums, in fire camps, in tents or hotels if traveling on a fire crew, or in a fire house. You might see them cleaning the sides of CA's roads, or working at a fair grounds, cleaning up a cemetery in your community, or many other community work assignments. It is not required that they be within a perimeter that is secure. They are the inmates who occasionally escape, they just walk away from their assigned place.

They may be guilty of multiple drunk drivings, petty theft, drug possession, securities violations, or a wide range of other non-violent felonies. If you live in CA you have probably done something, that if it had come to the authorities attention, could have gotten you placed into a Level I California prison.

Level II is for those inmates whose points range from 19 to 27. Chuckawalla Valley State Prison (CVSP) is a Level II and also houses some Level III "overrides". Overrides are offenders who because of their crime, say Manslaughter or Murder in the Third Degree, and serving Life with the Possibility of Parole, can never have points lower than a mandatory 28, but who have no history of disciplinary actions. They know how to behave themselves. Level II prisons have a secure perimeter, strong fencing, guard towers maned 24 hours a day 365 days a year, and at CVSP a

50

combination electrified fence with an "Israeli Wire" fence that is designed to wrap anyone attempting to climb it into a pipe of springy razor wire. No one in Corrections or the Governors Office wants to explain to a press conference why an inmate serving Life with the Possibility of Parole for Murder of some degree, or manslaughter, escaped from prison and is now on the loose. The nuances of the Classification Process are often lost in the headlines that appear in the Sacramento Bee and the Los Angeles Times.

Level III is for those inmates whose points range from 28 to 51, and Level IV is 52 and above. The computer system that is used to store the information on an inmates points is limited to three digits.

Ferrez, Taylor, Hymes, and Garza, and a small number of the other inmates exceed the 999 point limit almost completely from the points they accumulate from receiving disciplinary action based on their behavior

It takes a dedication to being a complete asshole to get to 999 points.

If an inmate is released before serving their entire term, because they miss behaved little enough while incarcerated, and this is the case for the vast majority of inmates, they are released on parole. They report to a parole officer and that system tracks them to some degree. A violation of parole will get you a fast ticket back to prison. Well it used to anyway, Jerry Brown's CA is not into punishing criminals.

When confined in SHU an inmate does not receive day for day, they receive no credit for time served off of the length of their sentence. But, the day does come from time to time when an inmate living in SHU has completed their original sentence for their crime. If all their misbehavior was of such a nature that they were never charged in a court with a new crime or if they have also served the time for any new crimes, they are free to go.

Hymes, with 999 points, and a history of violence in the community and while incarcerated, eventually served his entire sentence, Knowing this day was close was probably the biggest factor in his decision not to attack me on the day we got him out of that holding cell. Two Officers put him in a van, he was given $200.00 by you the taxpayer, was taken to the bus station in Crescent City, CA and when the bus pulled in the two Officers removed his handcuffs and that dangerous, sick, brain-dead, POS was free. He never did move to Crescent City or come over for bar-b-Que, he went home to Oakland.

Hymes did not stay free for long, not many parolees do, for the most part they are sociopaths, and even within your communities drug, and prostitution sub cultures, people fear them and are very willing to talk to police in an effort to get these scary monsters back behind bars.

I just spent about 45 minutes looking on the Internet for a story about one of PBSP's parolees who went on a murder rampage here in northern California the weekend he paroled, but my searching mostly lead to a lot of propaganda sites put up by inmate lovers. I dread the thought that someday my book will be a "hot" topic on news shows, because this section becomes relevant due to good people and hard working cops dying because of the system's blindness in letting these idiots loose.

And make no mistake, Taylor, Garza, Hymes, and Ferrez are far from the worst psychopaths locked up in CA's prisons, and they are harmless compared to the real dangerous inmates in PBSP and PBSP's SHU. Their ability to be a threat to you is not stopped because they are confined.

The Internet search turned up a couple of hits on a case that riveted the nation, one I planned to talk about, so maybe this is the time.

C-11's A-Section housed a number of Aryan Brotherhood (AB or Brand) members and associates. Gangs have hierarchies, with some variation on the Member and Associate theme. In the Italian Mafia becoming a member as called "being made". Made men, or Members are supposed

52

to have real power, gangs fill out their ranks with Associates, or Soldiers who aspire to become a Member someday. It is not really possible to know from the outside who has made it as a Member, but there are clues and at PBSP we really tried to figure it all out.

In C-11, on the lower tier Danny Troxell and Danny Christensen, "Danny T" and "Danny C" were housed in Cell 103. Danny C's parents were wealthy, they flew a twin engined plane they owned around the Pacific Ocean. Danny C studied Physics and got a degree while in his cell, he paroled, and he came back. So much for society oppressing felons.

I/M John "Youngster" Stinson, and his cellie I/M Terflinger were also in the unit. I don't remember where anymore. I well remember the day I saw Stinson in a debriefing unit walking around without hand cuffs. He was known to have killed with his bare hands. He talked to me about staying in shape and yoga because for years he had watched me working out in my control booth during slack times.

In C-11 cell 104 was Inmate Dale Bretches, one of the inmates involved in the infamous Dog Mauling case in San Francisco, CA when on January 26, 2001 Diane Whipple, a petite 34-year-old college lacrosse coach was killed by a vicious Presa Canarios dog.

The case brought Paul "Corn Fed" Snyder to the publics eye. Snyder eventually debriefed, or told law enforcement what he knew of AB and other gang activities, but only after the attention he brought to the Brand made him a liability to the AB, who "put him in the hat" or authorized his murder.

During the trial of the two Bay Area lawyers who had the dog in their apartment there were whispers of bestiality. The court refused to allow the subject to be brought up, but it didn't save Robert Noel and Marjorie Knoller, husband-and-wife attorneys who adopted Snyder in one of the cases many bizarre turns.

53

During the investigation of the crime, Bretches' cell was searched. In the cell were photos of the dog having sex with a woman, the woman was not Marjorie Knoller, instead it was a woman who lived in Hayfork, CA and had raised the dogs before the Knollers took them to the Bay Area. The judge in the case was probably correct in not allowing this information, but it does go a long way towards explaining the dogs attack. He was trained to have sex. Rumors have it that the dogs and various women are featured in porn videos too, a lot of porn is produced by gangs. When you mix meth and ruthless men, anything is possible.

"Corn Fed" Snyder was one of SHU's most dangerous inmates. He was found with weapons in his possession many times. His upper arms were bigger than my legs, and I have large muscular legs. For many many years he kept a wound on his leg festering and hid materials, maybe carbon steel or more likely diamond because it isn't found by a metal detector, that he used to cut the mild steel used in prison construction so he could make weapons.

Every evening he was escorted to a clinic and the wound dressed, but eventually he killed the bone and lost part of the leg. At one time I had the D-SHU Corridor Control Third Watch Relief position, I worked in the booth on Sunday and Monday nights. On Sunday evenings the two officers who would escort "Corn Fed" to the clinic during one period were two petite female officers. Paul Snyder was already known to have the ability to break handcuffs, many inmates were able to break them, and AB members were required to also carry makeshift keys that could open handcuffs too. When those two officers escorted Snyder I would sit at an equipment port with a Ruger Mini-14 .223 Rifle. Snyder knew it too. It was the only circumstance where I ever took that precaution.

On one occasion Snyder was found to have a knife taped to his body in his underarm. When I came on duty at 14:00 I was told to join a team and we escorted him to a new freshly searched cell. We used a metal detector on him, gave him new bedding and sanitary supplies, and new clothing. We took the t-shirt and boxers he wore during the escort too. They next afternoon I was ordered to search his cell with a team. The door frame of his cell had a 3/8ths inch thick rectangular piece of steel about seven inches long and two inches wide almost completely cut out of it. Paul Snyder is now in a Federal Penitentiary protected from the other members of the Brand who he knows are fully capable of killing him, despite his own dangerous skills.

The AB killed many of their own. Most of the killings at PBSP were done by an AB's cellie. The AB required each member to practice with garrotes made by braiding strips torn from sheets. As an AB you had to let your cellie put a garrote around your neck, it showed you were loyal. These murders by cellie would eventually lead to the majority of the SHU inmates being single celled, destroying their love lives.

I don't know all the stories or names of the many AB's killed in SHU or on PBSP's main line. But, I do know the story of Ruffo. I/M Ruffo was a dull normal individual, and he was strangled to death on Feb 17, 1996 by AB Associate Bryan "Dead Eye" Healy, on orders from AB Member John Stinson. I know Healy well, I shot him once. Healy was young and aggressive and hoped to someday become an AB Member.

When I became C-11 Control, Healy was single celled, because of the murder, in B- Section Upper Tier Cell 208 awaiting trial.

On June 1, 1997 I/M Healy came back from court after I had finished showers in C-11. I had put I/M Goldie, a Northern Mexican Gang Member onto the exercise yard. There was enough time before chow to shower Healy. He used the lower tier shower. When he came out of the shower I closed it. I took the small red key we used to open doors electronically from the booth and went to put it into the position for cell 208, the nearest hole to that one is the position for opening the exercise yard door. In a split second, during a quiet moment, I made my careers big mistake. I opened the exercise yard door by accident.

I/M Goldie charged into B- Section from the yard and went to tackle Healy who was wearing flip flop shower shoes, boxers and a T-shirt. Goldie wanted to fight Healy inside the section because if the fight was on the yard I could not provide gun coverage. I shouted, "O shit" which got the attention of Officers Brian Kiler and Jason Pebles sitting at the Floor Officers station. I grabbed a Mini-14 and a 38 millimeter (38MM) Gas Gun, and stepped up to the observation window. Right below me Inmate Healy was finishing a punch to Goldie's head. Goldie was on his back under Healy. Healy made a move to try and slam Goldie's head against the pavement. Make no mistake about it, killing Goldie would be a feather in Healy's cap, and my mistake might be enough to get him off of his murder rap. It might also get either or both of them wounded or killed. In this circumstance, with the possibility of a murder happening because of my mistake, it was still my responsibility to use my force options to bring an end to the fight. My options were the less than lethal 38MM , or the Ruger Mini-14's .223 caliber 50 grain bullets at @ 3500 feet per second. While the .223 is a low powered rifle round, it is capable of killing men.

The 38MM holds a 1.5 inch aluminum shell with 5 round rubber disks that are propelled by a charge of black powder. It is a single shot weapon. Policy dictated that I "skip" the rubber rounds into the inmates. Since they were almost directly below me it looked like a waste of time to try. Current CDCR Use of Force Policy would allow me to use "alternate force options" and if deadly force was appropriate I could aim the 38MM directly at the inmates. But, currently the 38MM is a thing of the past and instead a 40MM "Direct Impact" round is used, it is a sponge rubber projectile, and I have used them to break up fights. They are not anywhere as effective as a skipped rubber round.

I chose to fire the 38MM into the floor about 6 inches

away from the two inmates. Every one of the 5 projectiles hit Healy. One near his shin and then each subsequent rubber disk striking higher up on his body until the last one sliced open his forehead above his left eye. No, this is not how he got the AKA "Dead Eye", but it almost made it ironically true. As I reloaded the gun I started to tear up and to cough, I thought to myself that black powder was a bitch in a small space.

I did not know right away that Officers Kiler and Pebles were making history. At that moment they became the first Officers to use Oleo-capsicum (Pepper Spray) AKA OC on inmates in PBSP SHU. Until them Sgt's or above had used either Mace or OC. At the time, policy for Officers was that you dispersed no more than 3 one second bursts of Pepper Spray from the MK-3 dispenser. Within a couple of years the rules were relaxed to the point that the only limit was at the point were the inmate might drown in the stuff. Over the years I have had the experience of being sprayed many times while battling inmates. It sucks.

The combination of Pepper Spray and the 38MM round ended the fight. I put Healy into the upper shower, opening his cell door might have allowed him to retrieve a weapon, and Goldie then backed up to the pod door for handcuffing. The situation under control, I began to feel like shit.

Day room is a program on the Main Line where all of a section's inmates are released in the evening to socialize. They play games and cards and talk. It sometimes goes bad and the inmates fight. In SHU the policy is no inmates who are not celled together are ever to be allowed to be in the same space, cell, shower yard or section, unless handcuffed and escorted. In SHU a "Day room" is a mistake that results in that policy being violated. It is always an error by a Control Booth Officer. The inmates don't always fight. But if they don't you have dodged a bullet. I guess I opened the wrong doors on half a dozen occasions, but that first one was the only one that resulted in a day room. The use of Pepper

Spray by Officers was not the only first from that event.

Officers too receive disciplinary action. There are a number of levels, starting with verbal instruction like Sgt. Remat had given me, ranging right up to prosecution and prison sentences. The lowest level of written action is a letter of contact, to document verbal instruction. The next harshest is a Letter of Instruction, or LOI.

An EL O EYE used to be proof you messed up good. Officers who have never had one dread getting one. I received three during my years at PBSP. The one I received for this day room was the first time an Officer received one for a day room in SHU. Opening thousands and thousands of doors a year, a control booth officer is going to make mistakes. You do all you can to concentrate, develop habits, and techniques to avoid it, but the saying among officers is there are two types of Officers, those with stories about mistakes, and liars.

Guard T K Ridges had LOI's in such huge numbers that he had wall papered his Control Booth with them. His Old School Approach made him a lot of enemies. One day on Second Watch I/M Hymes started attacking his escorts while in the hallway in front of C-Corridor Control. Guard Ridges was ordering him to stop by yelling "Stop" and he was striking Hymes with his PR-24 Side-handle Baton. I/M Hymes had clamped his jaws down on another staff member, like a mad animal, and would not stop biting them. Program Administrator (PA) Doggy Whosez, who was also known as "The Head of the EME" by Correctional Staff, started yelling "Stop" also. He later said he was yelling at Ridges whom he said was violating policy. PA Whosez had it out for Guard Ridges.

After the incident was over PA Whosez alleged that Guard Ridges was using excessive and unnecessary force. A female Lt had returned to her office and written her version of the incident accurately. But PA Whosez convinced her to throw out that report and write one that made it look like Ridges was disobeying Whosez's orders to stop. Guard Hegel

58

retrieved her original report from the trash.

It was a huge national news story when that evening PBSP in coordination with the Del Norte County Sheriff went to T K Ridges home and arrested him. They claimed he had beaten I/M Hymes and wouldn't stop when ordered to do so. The report Hegel retrieved saved TK from going to prison, but of course the lying Administrators got off scott free for their obvious unmoral behavior. Business as usual. Of course all the Correctional Officers said, see don't be outspoken like TK, they will get you. Guards just said, "Man TK is a cool dude."

Doggy Whosez is a piece of work. At one time all the top EME (Southern Mexican) gang leaders were housed in D-7 E Section. "E" section for "EME". Cute. That was Doggy Whosez's idea, he would say it was easier to keep an eye on them. Bull Shit, it was easier for them to be powerful.

At one time my job included two nights as the Floor Officer in D-7. The big hassle was the huge volume of mail being received by the EME in the unit. It was not just E-pod, but the whole unit was heavy with EME inmates. By flooding the mail they overwhelmed the Floor Officers, many of whom were unable to do a thorough job of searching the mail for drugs, coded messages, and metals like foil that could be used to disguise the removal of razor blades from the disposable razors. A small strip of foil can easily look like a razor blade under the cap of a disposable razor. In those days there were no magnets in the units to test the razors.

I also had one of the two weekly laundry nights in the unit. On one night dirty laundry went out, and on another the clean laundry returned. Because laundry was cleaned by inmates, conscientious Guards searched the Laundry for contraband: weapons, messages, drugs, even food, it all was passed from the main line inmates to the SHU inmates. In the outgoing laundry they sent messages.

Now messages may not sound important. But, that was how the gang conducted business. It ordered hits,

59

appointed leaders, coordinated drug deals, and planned the harassment of Officers who were conscientious to try to cow them into becoming lazy, their chief helpers in this were the administrators. "Why are these inmates always complaining about you." - because I do my J. O. B.

Holiday

On Christmas Eve in D-7 I walked in to find that some misguided Christian organization had delivered the Inmates Christmas Candy in a bulk box. They had left it to the officers to but it into paper sacks. Well it certainly was not my priority, in the past they had carried the paper sacks right to the cells with one Officer escorting them, or had at least delivered it in the sacks.

I started on the mail and the laundry. Immediately I found items in the laundry so I had to write a report. I could have just thrown the stuff away and continued, but that was not my job, it was my job to write the incident up. Then I went to an alarm.

I came back and started in on the huge pile of mail, and the laundry. And was making headway when it became chow time. As we fed the inmates were relentless, "Where is the mail, where is the laundry where is the candy you fucker." It isn't the best way to motivate me.

During chow I got a phone call to go to a Control Booth in another unit to relieve the Officer, so I went.

It transpired that Lt Helga was conducting an investigation into the way this unit fed inmates. It took about an hour and a half before I got back to my unit. We still had to pick up the dinner trays. The inmates attitude was worse. I was starting to feel like it was a real bitch of a Christmas Eve.

We got the trays and trash out, and while pushing them down the hallway the Sgt told me I should come to the "spread", our facility Christmas potluck. I said thank you but I was too busy and returned to my unit. I got the laundry out and the assholes were still bitching about candy and mail. I was working on the mail when my phone rang. It was the Sgt who told me I was ordered to come to the party. OMG.

So I left the mail and the candy and went to the party for just long enough to get a plate of food, see the Sgt and

61

say hi to Lt Helga. I went back to my unit with about an hour left to try and do the mail and get the candy out, though by now I was starting to think something was not going to get done, and the phone rang again.

I was ordered to the Lt's office. She wanted to know why I did not stay at the party. I told her about the work load of the evening and the work I left to do, and she ordered me to stay at the party. I was furious. I had to face the Inmates, not this dumb bitch. I doodled a rant on the back of a memo that had been in the mail while waiting for the count phone at 21:00 hours and then threw it in the trash. The mail and the candy were still on the carts when I left that evening.

The next day, Christmas, I went to work knowing I was going to take some heat. I was not prepared for the memo to be in the hands of Big Al Scribner, the SHU Program Administrator at that time.

But, it turns out Big Al is a good man. He listened to my side of the story. At one point he told me that other Officers believed the EME would have me attacked for not getting them their candy and mail. He said I could have any other job that administration could give me if I wanted to give up the one I had. Well I am not that guy. So I asked his permission to ask the EME straight up if they had a problem with me. I said I did not want another job, I wanted to do my job.

I walked down to D-7 and entered E-pod walking up to the cell of "Topo" Peters, a top EME Member. I asked him if I had any reason to be afraid of the EME, Now of course this was overstepping a lot of boundaries. He would never admit to there even being such a thing as La EME, nor could he presume to speak for all of them, nor go to bat for me against even one of them. He said he couldn't speak about that, but he did say he did not have a problem with me. He said there was someone on the upper tier I needed to talk to. To get to cell 217 I had to walk in front of every cell. In 217 was "Boxer" Enriquez. Later "Boxer" would be one of the highest ranking EME Members to debrief to Prison and other Law Enforcement authorities. Chris Blatchford wrote a book about him, <u>The Black Hand: The Bloody Rise and Redemption of "Boxer" Enriquez, a Mexican Mob Killer.</u>

But, on this day I didn't even know who he was. He gave me a little lecture, and I played humble. And, to this day I hate Lt Helga. Once upon a time after she had thrown a rigging fit she told a group of us that she knew she was being bad, and when she did it we should just say, "O Boyle" and she would laugh and calm down. When she walked away from us we all agreed that not a man among us had balls enough to pull that stunt. But, Boyle I would like to say now, fuck you.

Troubles

My second LOI would come some time later, I thought I had a swap that was to be repaid on Monday morning, a swap is an agreement between two officers where each officer works the others shift. On this Swap I had it wrong, the date I was supposed to work was a Sunday morning. The phone rang at about 6:10 in my house, and Sgt. Anthony asked me why I was not at work. When I realized my mistake I had a true dilemma.

I was doing this swap to have time off during the Del Norte County Fair. My three children took sheep, pigs, dairy heifers, springer heifers, steers and beef heifers and more to the fair. I was our clubs swine leader and that Sunday morning I had 75 young people taking their swine projects to auction.

I told Sgt Anthony my situation and said I was not going to be at work and I understood I would receive disciplinary action. When I hung up I hoped it would only be an LOI, and not a loss of pay or loss of swap privileges. My cousin Danny Forkner got held over to work my shift, to this day he tells everyone that I am the only guy he knows who told the prison I wasn't coming to do my swap because I wanted to go to the fair.

By this time, as I have explained already, I was doing up to 100 swaps each year. I worked as a relief officer on third watch in C-SHU. I did all my swaps in units C-2 through C-6. To discipline me by taking away my swap privilege would alter the vacation plans of a dozen other officers. Since it was fall, most of my swaps at that time had already been worked by me. It was almost hunting season.

When I was called a week later to come see Sgt. Anthony, I was pretty sick to my stomach. But, I was also used to standing up and being a man about my failings too. Sgt Anthony just had me sign the LOI, and then he said. What you did is wrong, but I like to think I would have made the same choice, don't let it happen again.

At one time it was like that. Managers did their job and they understood that everyone was human. Those days are long past, and even back then I got off easily mostly because I was a good solid conscientious officer. In later years my injuries would damage that reputation, but eventually I would be considered a solid member of the team again. Most officers have similar periods during their careers.

My third LOI illustrates an officer's daily duties and decisions pretty well. It was a busy night. I had worked Second Watch for an overtime, I was evolving away from doing tons of swaps because my feet were so bad, and also because my seniority was better and I could get days off and vacation when I wanted it in the fall. But, I was doing more overtimes to pay for traveling and to raise my children.

SHU was on lock down and being searched. In my unit it was Laundry night. I got the laundry ready to go during shift change and even though management was really adamant that officers not open any cuff and food ports while alone, I went through and handed the laundry bags through the ports. On a normal non lock down day the Control Booth would have used the porters to put the bags on the doors, and would have cracked each door in turn so the inmates could retrieve the bags.

In C-Section I/M Terry Haddix was in the last cell on the bottom tier, cell 112. When I got there he was mouthing off to me, and looked almost like he might gas me. In my whole career I was never gassed, I attribute this to three things, first a working relationship with inmates that was not based on my giving ground, they knew gassing me wouldn't have made me weaker and more prone to do things their way. Second I was aware. I always watched what inmates were doing, I am lucky to be situationally aware and it served me well over the years. Third I am one lucky son of a bitch.

One morning I was picking up trays from breakfast

with Guard Joe Joe Beeson. The inmate in front of me was taking his sweet time and I was just about to slam his port shut and call it a refusal, which would mean paperwork but would give him a lesson. Joe Joe came along and passed right behind me. He stopped at the next cell and received the worst gassing I ever saw, and I saw many of them from control booths, or saw the officer on their way to a shower. The inmate said he didn't have anything against Joe Joe or me, he had just decided that morning to gas the next person, staff, inmate, officer, doctor, Rabbi, or whomever, he didn't care, that stepped in front of his cell. Awareness and people skills will only take you so far, I am grateful to God for my luck, it is after all better to be lucky than to be good.

You know Terry Haddix. Almost all of the documentaries on PBSP show an Inmate doing bar dips on B-yard on a rainy day, and two other inmates in yellow rain gear approach him. One of them is wearing a Sou' Wester hat and he starts stabbing the inmate on the bar dips. The idiot with the knife is Terry Haddix. At one time he was a dangerous lunatic idiot. Now a days he is a model inmate because he claims to have found the lord during about three days when his balls were on fire from Pepper Spray. God works in wondrous ways, and I have seen the power of the Spray, PBSP has been transformed by Pepper Spray, and maybe someday we can use it on bad managers and politicians so they too can see the glory of good social skills.

So anyway, all the other inmates got their laundry and Haddix's laundry bag was left on the floor. We got called out to do searches and who knows what else, Haddix was fed through a special food port with a paper tray in those days due to some misbehavior or another so while we would have normally got him his laundry during chow it just didn't happen, he was probably still screaming at us too. It was a typical routine for him.

I went in to count at 21:00, one hour before we got off shift and there was the bag. I sighed, time to practice my skills. I picked up the bag and asked him, can you behave long enough for me to open your port and give you your bag. In almost 100% of these situations an inmate would be ready to give up on the war for today, take his laundry, and fight again tomorrow wearing clean boxers. I stood to the side when I opened the port so when Haddix tried to grab at my belt I was able to jump away without there being any real danger. But, now I was pissed off.

So I went and wrote a 115 to make sure I/M Haddix was disciplined. I knew full well I was about to get in trouble myself for opening the port alone. But, Haddix would never know I got in trouble, and since it was my third LOI, I was used to the pain by now.

67

Sean

Sometimes it is funny the way you encounter the same inmates over time. One of the strangest ones for me was I/M Shawn Bromley an A/B Associate. Bromley saw himself as a rising star in the Aryan Brotherhood. He was barrel chested and confrontational.

I was walking into SHU one afternoon and was conversing with Lt Crandall. I asked about her new assignment to the gangs unit. She said it was very interesting because, "Number two always wants to be number one, and they all think they are number two."

I forget the details of my first meeting with Bromley, but I know I wrote him up. I am a believer in nipping trouble in the bud, and he was trouble. It came to my attention that he is married to a much older woman who is one of the Del Norte County's heroin suppliers. Personally I am no drug warrior, the drug war itself is destroying Liberty in the world. However, Bromeley's wife lived in the same neighborhood as my ex-wife and children.

Bromley felt like an up and coming AB because he was getting drugs into PBSP. His wife would send him tons of mail, much of it just colored construction paper. Officers knew that this had to be the vehicle for introducing drugs into the prison, but the sheer volume, reams and reams of paper, made stopping it difficult.

I was working as the second watch floor officer in D-8 and Bromley was housed in D-8 cell 112. He was on his way out to some appointment or other one day, and I searched his cell. It was filed with colored paper. When he came back I told him to get rid of it, it exceeded the 6 cubic feet of possessions an inmate can have in a cell, and it was a potential source of material for arson. Bromley did not like me, or anyone, telling him what to do. His response was disrespectful. I resolved to make a special effort to see if I could stop his drug smuggling.

68

I had rashly made life difficult for the third watch floor officer in the unit, and had already decided to make amends. So when he got there that afternoon I apologized for being petty, then I told him of my interaction with Bromley. He said he hoped we could work together to stop the massive mail load. Things happened quickly after that discussion.

The next day Bromley left his cell to go to the dentist. I went into C-section and started searches. In all the cells I found colored paper. And, thanks be to god, in the cell of a heavy Southern Mexican, Cell 111 right next to Bromley, there was a small manila envelope with loose pages of naked women, pornography. Now if there is one thing I really don't care about is inmates having pornography. I can not believe it isn't allowed to begin with, but this porn was heaven sent.

I really left this Hispanic inmates house in a mess. As soon as he was returned to his cell he wanted to talk to me. He asked, politely what was the reason I tore his cell up. I calmly told him it was the colored paper. That his neighbor Bromley was a drug smuggler and that we had talked to him about all the colored paper. I told him it was my new mission in life to bring an end to the colored paper. I showed him that I had the envelope of porn, and then I slid it back to him under his cell door.

When I came to work the next day Bromley was gone. I talked to the third watch cop and he said when he came to work the night before Bromley had been in a panic and insisted he had to move out of that unit for his own safety.

One of the repercussions to him was that, his wife kept sending his mail to his old cell. And, it had to be re-routed every day. This meant a delay in his receiving it. It must have also disrupted his receiving messages from other AB members. His old wife missed a meeting with I/M Frank Clements wife. I/M Clements is an AB Member, his ire over the missed meeting was a career killer for up and comer Bromley.

Inmates get to visit their families on weekends. The next Saturday I was escorting I/M Clements to visiting and other officers were escorting I/M Bromley. Bromley saw Clements but did not notice me. In a panic he was apologizing to Frank. He was trying desperately to make amends so he could keep his status, keep his wife in the drug business, and maybe even save both of their lives. Frank Clement is not a man you want to have disappointed in you.

Now by this time I was very in tune with Bromley and his situation. I wrote a long report about the conversation between Clement and Bromley. Under normal circumstances we escorting officers would have made them not talk to one another, but this opportunity was so obvious that none of the other officers said a word. The brief glimpse into the AB's workings was very valuable. In just a week Bromley realized that he was now a target to be killed by the AB, he was in the hat. So much for being an up and comer. He debriefed and went into the rat program. But, he kept dealing drugs.

I changed jobs on a regular basis at PBSP. I used to tell my self it was for better days off. But, now I know I just did not like being there. I started working as the Transitional Housing Unit (THU) floor officer on Sundays, the day THU went to visit their families at visiting. One day a returning inmate yelled across the yard to some kitchen inmates that "Shawn" had seen his wife that day and things were cool. I notified the security squad and a raid on THU proved Bromley was smuggling drugs to B-Yard.

By now Bromley was under the impression that I was being sent to ruin his life. I had one other interaction with Bromley. My last job at PBSP was as acting Correctional Counselor (CCI(A)). One of my duties was finding THU inmates transfers to other prisons. But Bromley was trying to stay at PBSP. He claimed a hardship because his wife was in Crescent City, she was sick, etc. He really worked it. But, I knew his history of having her aid him with his drug smuggling. I did not get all that many transfers approved during that time, but I did get one for Bromley.

Day Rooms

There are two other day room incidents I was involved in that are worth mentioning. When I had two years into the department I had taken the exam for promotion to Sargent. On the day the results came out I was working with Rich Xilliams. He got a phone call and then he told me that he had placed in the second rank and I had placed in the third and the next person at PBSP was in the fifth rank. He walked over to the Program Services Office and came back wearing Sargent's chevrons on his collar, and handed me a state application, "Fill it out and turn it in tomorrow and your promoted." It was his first action as a Sargent. I never promoted, but for my entire career Rich and I always worked well together.

On the day that I got to help Robin Roast with the I/M Brown problem the first of the three alarms I went to was a day room. I was just walking past the unit when the alarm went off. I ran in to see two inmates behind the stairs at the back of that units C-Section fist fighting. Sgt. Rich Xilliams showed up and grabbed a gas gun, I started handing him ammunition and sent another officer for more of it.

The Lt. I had left in Hymes cell showed up. He started chewing Rich Xilliams out because I had a bunch of ammo on the floor. I was knelled down, handing Rich ammo. The Lt. was yelling at us, which was really ludicrous because everyone knows Rich is as deaf as a rock, and the alarm was still ringing, as fast as I could hand him rounds and he could load, Rich was firing away at the two inmates. I am being nice to this Lt. and not mentioning his name, because I know him to be a kind person, but he was a horrible supervisor. He often mentioned we should go hiking or hunting together, it never happened.

He should have been directing the POS Officers that also responded. They never did anything to help, and I ended up in the control booth as the extra gunner in a couple of minutes. My report was not well received because of my criticism of the POS's.

The last day room is, I think, as bad as one can be without someone being actually injured. Officer Mole was the Control Booth cop, instead of being a Guard or CO, or even a Correctional Officer and getting the yards put away knowing chow was coming, he waited like a POS to the last second to give the inmates more time. And, my feeling is if you can manage doing multiple tasks then go ahead, you are in Control after all. But for him it was just bad decision making.

Tony Slybony and I were feeding the unit. Tony is one of my favorite people. Happy, humorous and at the same time aware and conscientious. A man I am happy to be friends with. We were in B- Section,

Tony had carried trays to the upper tier and I was feeding the bottom tier, when I heard a door open upstairs. I stepped back and looked up. Cell 207's door was open and the inmate was looking out at Tony, I yelled at Cole, but since the inmate was calm I kept my voice calm too.

Tony handed the inmate a tray, I started to go up the stairs, but now both 106 and 107, right in front of me were opening. It was now five inmates and the two of us, I knew two of the cells were Southern Gang Members and one cell was Northern Structure Gang, a volatile mixture. Tony was trying to get Mole's attention, I glanced at Mole, he was facing C-Section and was busily turning knobs, cell 206 opened, seven to two.

I screamed at the top of my lungs, "We don't need anymore doors open in here." Mole was so startled he jumped, then he looked into our section, where he should have been focused all along, and by some miracle he got the doors closed. The true miracle is they got closed without the inmates coming out after us. We finished feeding the pod and exited.

Tony was livid, he was calling Mole every name in the book. He put one arm up and grabbed an iron bar that

72

separated the rotunda from the control booth and chinned his head up against the bars, his right arm was above his head, fist clenched. "Come her you motherfucker, let me get my hands on you." I got him down from the bars, he said what are we going to do? I said we are going to finish feeding the unit.

I asked mole if he had all the inmates locked up, and he said yes, so I said open C-section,and he did.

And then, he said it, becoming a POS for all time in my book, "I don't know why your worried, I have a gun." I had to push Tony into C-section.

An apology, any acknowledgement that he was sorry for putting our lives at risk, anything of that sort would have made a world of difference. But you can't fix stupid, and that Mole is at risk of an ass whipping to this day. Because if I get the chance I am going to show that idiot how the Guards used to do it. But, I was not willing to tell on him and have him receive an LOI, and he was not man enough to tell on himself.

Bradford

Some of the time a rough justice would emerge in prison. I mentioned Doggy Whosez in a couple incidents, but one incident is known far and wide about Doggy, and it is classic.

My cousin Sally Gal would eventually fall in love with and marry my brothers brother in law. And since he was doing life without that relationship ended her career as a Correctional Officer. But before that happened she would shoot I/M Bradford.

I/M Bradford was a classic inmate from the same mold as Hymes, Taylor, Garza, and Ferez. A constant source of trouble, violence, and stress.

One day he came out of his cell with a cup of shit and piss and started walking toward the control booth. Sally did not know if he was going to throw it at her, or into one of the other cells, so she used her 38MM Federal Gas Gun to apply less lethal force.

Now some administrators saw this as unnecessary force. And chief among them was Doggy Whosez. So Gal was under investigation, and the whole prison wondered how much trouble she was in, if any.

Doggy Whosez decided he would be the one to do the hearing of Bradford over the fact that he was threatening others by having his cup of piss and shit out on the tier. Now since I/M Bradford was such a problem to deal with, and Doggy was elevating him to the status of saint so he could get a guard, Gal, in trouble, Doggy decided to hold the hearing in the pod in front of Bradford's cell.

When the little hearing group showed up and asked to go into the pod, Gal who was in the Control Booth warned Doggy that the floor staff had told her Bradford had another cup o shit. Doggy's classic response was, "Gal, Bradford would never gas staff."

Officers and our bargaining Unit CCPOA are always

upset that the system never takes inmates to court when they assault us by gassing us with piss and shit. But, they did take Bradford to court for gassing Doggy Whosez and the Captain he had with him. Cute.

The Team

Prison is a team sport. Obviously the green team –
Custody staff, in our green jumpsuits, or our tan shirts and
green pants, plain for day to day Guard work, stripped and
bedecked for those who promote or interact out in public.
But, also red ties and business suits for the "Specialists" and
"Associates", the Wardens and Business Services Captains,
and well the list is nearly endless.

This team in theory is all of society: united in
keeping evil, dangerous, or just stupid and self-centered
felons out of our communities, away from our children and
grand parents, our young boys and girls, all of us who don't
prey on one another, or at least those whose predations are
codified by the legislature as evil and wrong.

It is a big team in theory, but it is a very fine pointed
spear, and the tip, where I stood, is easily bent, not just from
the resistance of the target, but from the shear mass of the
spear and the blade. And while I believe our team was very
sharp 15 years ago, today the mass has broken it down, and I
grew weary of trying to do fine work with a dull knife.

American justice is far removed from the "Justice"
our Nation was founded to promote, that shining vibrant
Justice of men ordering their affairs through the dictates of
their conscious.

Never have I been able to see myself as a Drug
Warrior, saving the world from weed and weirdness.

Watch a cop show on American Television these
days, and even more so the Wildlife War drivel, and you see
how wrong headed the police have become. And, if you get a
close look at the Courts, Prosecutors, Judges, and Lawyers,
like I did, a thinking, caring individual finds it hard to be a
cog in the wheels of "justice".

It is said a lawyer in a small town will starve, but two
can do rather nicely. Well add the power to fine the citizen,
and the threat of putting you in prison if you refuse to plea

bargain, and let's just say you can't arrive at truth when your only desire is to win at all costs.

Into the rain I went, the ground soaked, the air filled with rain and mist, my good dog along for the adventure. I hobbled on one good leg, my left alternating between being a boon lifelong companion and shooting daggers of agony up my ankle. The two black Angus steers Tom and I bought a couple of weeks ago were standing in the lean-to, waiting for the heaps and heaps of expensive grain. I endure the agony of paying for feeding them, because the quality of the meals I will enjoy later is real enough to bring me to salivating as I think of it now.

Feeding cows is so much more rewarding than feeding inmates. Every day, meal after meal, week after week, month after month, year in year out, since before homo-sapien's Neanderthal brothers disappeared, and forward until the sun is extinguished, the incarcerated man tortures his jailer. "My cookies broken, what are you going to do about it?", "There is only one snack in my lunch!", "Would you eat a banana like this one?" "What are you going to do about it." "What are you going to do about it." "What are you going to do about it." "Fuck you motherfuckers."

Nothing! In the short run and the long run what I plan to do about it is nothing. They embraced liberalism and socialism and as a man who rejects that failure, I am unafraid to let them enjoy the bitter fruit, I am not afraid to let them fail. Rage all you want, I am not lifting a finger to lessen your pain. I am unsure how you got to where you are, but I know how it can be avoided. And, it isn't that hard to do.

The inmates are a team too, and the gangs with their ties into every level of society, from the Chicago gangster in the White House running guns to Mexican Cartels and Muslim Extremists to fuel a narrative that guns are too dangerous for America to tolerate, through the leftists in the universities, and the fretful, reading the liberal papers at Starbucks, right on down to the children in the barrios, their team is supported by kings, knaves, puppets and soldiers who never care about the consequences to individuals. They don't grieve for the dead liquor store owner, the old woman raped and robbed, the teenager gunned down for being on the wrong corner wearing the wrong shoes. They never connect the dots. But, the warriors have no choice. If you can not connect the dots in SHU, you will be victimized.

Extractions are scary: dangerous and scary. When the cell door rolls open what is that convicted murderer going to do? He knows that any damage he does to you, short of murder, won't get him one more minute of time in prison. If he is doing life without parole he knows that even murdering you may not lengthen his sentence. It might even get him to San Quentin State Prison's Death Row, where life is more fun for an inmate than it is in the heavily controlled environment of SHU.

It is a sad thought for a Guard, that your death would make your killers life more interesting. He would get to go out to court. There would be attractive women to look at in the court house, some would smile at him. The media would drag up ancient allegations that Guards are evil, and your children would go hungry.

So

I find myself still inside the prisons I created to mask the horror and stress of life inside prison. To you they look like hobbies: my ranching, boats, hiking, shooting, and this writing. Right now I don't find the joy in them I used to, they are no longer an escape from something, and so the central meaning of them is lost. The central meaning of me, the need to be a survivor is lost right now. My only struggle is with the American Police State and its purposeful destruction of the dollar.

It is gut wrenching to bring all the sickness back into my mind. My cousin Reggie Loftin was here last night, he spoke of one incident of CDCR injustice, I have notes on cocktail napkins as the stories come back while I am out trying to eat. A spiral note book rests at my elbow.

My local newspaper has a PBSP story on the front page, "Pelican Bay's Lewis loses 'interim' label". That silly headline means that PBSP's acting Warden has been confirmed by the State of California to now become a full Warden.

On the one hand I don't really know the man, and judge not and you shall not be judged, on the other, this interview is like a snapshot of a crime scene, evidence of all that is wrong with prison, government, and this modern era.

So why do prisons exist, not all societies have seen the need for them, why are ours overflowing? PBSP exists according to its mission to house the most dangerous inmates in California. Which is like saying my kitchen exists to store food. The major purpose of PBSP is to continue the War on Drugs. The number of men in prison who are not there because of the war on drugs must be very small. Look at how any murder of a wife by a husband becomes a national headline story, unless she is black, poor, and possibly unattractive. But drug war fueled gang killings barely make the back pages of newspapers anymore.

79

We see hundreds of stories of Government graft and malfeasance, yet I can only name one politician I know is in prison right now: "Blago".

Some would say that prisons are a way to control minorities. The percentage of minority individuals in the prison system is staggering, I think 25% of African American males go to prison.

I have been known to say that White inmates must be pretty dumb on average, because it is not easy for white guys to get sent to prison. But the way I see it, the tool used to lock up so many men is the Drug War. Progressives invented it, and some how conned conservatives into overlooking their belief in Liberty and limited government, and convinced them to embrace Tyranny and a huge para military force operating a guerrilla war on American soil. The Drug Warriors ignore property rights, have destroyed the concept of probable cause, and have made it possible for anyone with a ruthless heart to destroy anyone else they want to. The Drug War has filled our California prisons at huge expense.

I firmly believe there isn't anything drugs do to individuals or families that is worse than what the "justice" system does.

For the most part it is the creation of a black market that creates the culture of drug use. Since it is illegal it is unregulated, so it is easy to get into and you can focus your time on manufacture and distribution. It interacts, or dovetails nicely with the welfare system. You have people who get a fixed income guaranteed, plus the ability to earn commissions, it makes the perfect work from home business.

Many people think drug users are a small percentage of America, they are crazy. The money pouring into the drug industry comes from all levels of American life, billions and billions comes from occasional users. Maybe they smoke a little pot on the annual canoe trip with the girls, or snort a line of coke before going to see the Chippendale dancers. The thing is though, the money flows to the most ruthless people.

Why we can watch the History Channel and see the lessons of Prohibition illustrated so clearly, and then make the same mistake, at huge cost in misery and resources is a puzzle to me. The worst part of it is that in a nation that is not supposed to base government on religion, the real quandary is the way drugs are portrayed as an evil: A moral argument.

The toll on our Liberty that the Drug War madness extracts weights heavy on my mind. I was the first on my block to have a "Ron Paul for President" sign. But I fear Americans won't be free until a Civil War either destroys the Federal leviathan, or ends with Liberty crushed. I stockpile food and ammo.

Hillary Clinton famously said, "It takes a village to raise a child." That is true, and the global, government, democratic progressive village only produces children. I baby sat them in PBSP for many years. It takes a family to raise an adult.

Correctional Officers have skin in the game, they literally keep the peace. I see no justice left in America. My time in the Justice system showed me it is all dog eat dog and power and circumstances, and it is worsening. You have to be imprisoned to lose your freedom, but we have all been deprived of our Liberty.

Workman's Compensation

My career was defined in my mind by the interaction I had with the Workman's Compensation Insurance Fund – why insurance is so hated is beyond me. It is simple, if a person is hurt working the employer is responsible.

But, the State Fund propaganda states that employee claims are mostly fraud. I have been through the Fund and PBSP administration's insinuation that I was defrauding them, and their attitude is despicable.

To demonstrate their predisposition I always mention two posters they had on the walls at PBSP: One poster said, "Liar, Con Artist, Co-worker, Thief." and the other poster said, "Workers Comp is an Attitude." The message is, if you make a claim of injury you are despicable.

They cannot point out any statistics that are hard facts, they weasel word the claim of fraud by saying "suspected of" and "estimates". In fact they consistently lose their attempts to deny claims based on fraud in court, and they spend a fortune second and third guessing Physicians and Psychiatrists who are treating injured workers.

I am only speaking here of injuries to Officers, not the whole system. My opinion is though they treat other workers even worse, because Unit 6 members have high salaries and the lawyers love to defend us. And, I believe it should be the law that all State Fund cases be automatically given an attorney for the injured worker.

My friend Tommy Tsunami has gone three years with 2 knees that need replacement and two different injured parts of his spine. One of the knees has been replaced, but month after month goes by without State Fund acting at all to allow him to get the rest of the medical attention he needs. And this is in a case where they have already admitted fault.

In my case the level of care provided was pitiful. They would approve orthotics, which in my experience are

82

less useful than witchcraft. In fact once I was retired over my feet I went to good Doctor, and he fixed my feet in two months, and told me that I don't have flat feet, I have a normal arch. Why the State Fund bums said otherwise is beyond me. They also perpetuated a myth that implies it is harder to walk on rough ground than on concrete. This is completely backwards. The rough ground uses different muscles and tendons, the concrete has you repeat the same motion continuously overworking and damaging a few tendons.

       Meanwhile at work, if you don't stay away from work for three days when you get injured, then the time you take off comes out of your sick leave account. They say it is so you don't make a false claim, bit has the effect of making sure people stay out more days. In fact since you can't come back after three days until you get a physicians note, and it takes State Fund forever to get you an appointment: you could show up at a doctors after healing in minor injury cases, then they scream fraud.

       When I was hurt originally I had the Cowboy John Wayne attitude that I would just work through it. So for three years I got worse, and suffered, and burned up my own sick leave. The whole time my bosses hated me. They of course never talk about your injury to your face. But, over the years you hear them say everyone who was hurt is faking it, so you know they think it of you too. "Workers Comp is an Attitude", a bad attitude on the part of everyone who isn't injured.

Riots

Pelican Bay is famous for its riots. I was never there for the really big ones. At first PBSP experienced them constantly. Later they would happen sporadically, but during certain periods they happened daily. My most regular role was as a responder from SHU, We would jump into a response van, donning helmets we scooped up Lexan shields, grabbed gas masks and vests loaded with gas grenades, multi launchers for 40MM baton and foam rounds, huge pepper spray canisters, bags full of plastic handcuffs and snips to remove them or just unholstered our batons and regular pepper spray containers.

I did the work of a responder. Backing up the lines, cuffing groups of inmates who had stopped rioting and were laying face down, cleared classrooms and chapels, often securing them as blood soaked crime scenes. I escorted nurses who had no clue what to do through clusters of inmates who all needed to be examined for injuries both from having been attacked and from fighting themselves, over yards white with chemicals used to disrupt and end the rioting.

It was riots where the MTA's had always been so valuable, as a combination Peace Officer and Medical specialist they knew what to do, and could do it with minimal help. When they were replaced by nurses the nurses were as useful in a riot, just as you would expect. Nice people, good at nursing, not so good at riot control. Thanks a bunch progressives.

One of my worst moments as it pertains to situational awareness was a riot day on B-yard. I was working as a CC-I the entry level Correctional Counselor level in Unit B-4. I was on my way out of the unit. I had a two wheel cart with boxes of files on it and I walked over to the exit and called up to the Control Officer to let me out. In a split second I saw through the window of the unit's door inmates swinging at each other. I heard gas guns being fired, the blare of the PA systems as Officers all over the yard and in the gunner positions yelled "Get Down" the lawful order we have to chant like a mantra while we use force.

B-yard at that time started at B-4, B1 through B-3 are the Psychiatric Services Unit (PSU),and B-3 had one of its three sections converted into the Transitional Housing Unit (THU) were the rats lived, I mean where the inmates who debriefed and gave up their gang affiliations lived.

All main line units have an area between two of them that was originally a chow hall and satellite kitchen. Because inmates are scum it proved impossible to let them eat in a chow hall at PBSP. Half of them were converted to other uses. Offices for medical and psychiatric staff was the main use for them. The kitchen between B-3 and B-4 was still used to prepare food and as the riot broke out the dozen inmates in the kitchen were ordered to get down when I reminded their supervising officer. The two officers in B-4 and I went into the kitchen and I took the lead in getting them down on the floor.

I should have continued to make sure this little area was secured. But, I had already been on my way out. I went on through the kitchen and had the B-3 Control Officer let me outside. A fence separated B-3 from the Main Line Yard. So I walked up to the program area of B-yard and helped officers secure the classroom. My main role was in stopping a POS teacher from handing the inmates folders of their school work. The possibility always exists that the inmate may have a weapon hidden in such a folder or something else, a coat, a book, a lunch bag. This dumb shit was handing these things to inmates even as the Officers were trying to stop him. I made it clear I would pepper spray him and cuff him up if he did it anymore. I would have, of course, lost my job if I did those things, but at least the dumb shit looked at my tie and thought I had more authority than the Guards in the room and stopped. I of course had less authority than the Guards in that situation, but liberals don't know shit from

85

shinola. Anyway, I got him stopped.

As soon as we got the school inmates outside and sitting handcuffed against a wall, the alarm sounded in the kitchen I had been in. A northern gang inmate rushed southern gang inmates, if he had not done so he would have been in trouble with his gang for not participating in the riot. He had only delayed because he had not known it was a Northern verses Southern riot until that moment.

If I had done my J. O. B., and acted like the experienced correctional professional I should have been at that point in my career, I would have had all those kitchen inmates secured in their cells before I had left that are. Technically it was not my responsibility, but morally I know better, and still see that day as One of my low points.

On B-Yard I responded to a couple of small riots, under 50 or 60 inmates. I generally secured the Chapel or the Law Library. I never used force during a riot. In fact my uses of force during my career were limited.

I already mentioned the use of a gas gun in SHU. I also used a gas gun in B-3 Control one afternoon. I was the THU officer when two inmates in the Transitional Placement Unit (TPU) which was the program in B-3's A and B Sections attacked a third inmate. I fired a couple of foam rounds – it was a typical gas gun use and not memorable. I never sprayed pepper spray, because in those situations I generally drew my baton or more likely would take an inmate to the ground to restrain him.

I must have put inmates on the ground scores of times. On a half dozen occasions other responding staff pepper sprayed me while trying to spray the inmate I was restraining. I know in one case the Officer got into trouble for unnecessary use of force, but they must have given themselves up, because I never mentioned it in any of the occurrences.

The time the officer got in trouble had some twists to it. A group of Officers and I were walking out of A-2, an Ad-Seg unit, when the alarm went off in A-3. We ran to respond

86

and on the yard in front of A-3 A guard was on top of a black inmate with a handcuff on one of the inmates wrists. A group of Hispanic kitchen workers were standing about 10 feet behind them. I was worried about their intentions and took a moment to order them down while pointing pepper spray at them, they complied.

I dove on top of the black inmate and got a hold of his un handcuffed arm. I saw the other Guard was bleeding from a blow to his nose, the inmate had hit him. Suddenly a canister of pepper spray was next to my face, I turned my face away but still took a solid shot of pepper spray. With my eyes closed and my lungs on fire I finished handcuffing I/M Browning. Then I stood him up and escorted him across the yard to a shower where he could get the pepper spray off of him. I turned him over to others and decontaminated myself in a bathroom.

I then learned who I/M Browning was. My brother in law Robert Broadbent won the CDC's Gold Star when three chicken shit black inmates attacked him on B-yard. Even though Robert was wounded from the knifes they used he subdued and cuffed one of the inmates before responding staff arrived and got the other two off of him.

A couple of days after I learned who Browning was, I was doing an overtime in B-3. As we relieved Second Watch they told us Browning had been acting out since his latest assault, and wanted someone to come in and hear his latest complaint. I volunteered.

I walked up to his cell and he started a typical inmate rant, I asked him to listen for a second, asked him if I was right about him being one of Broadbent's assailants. Of course he did not admit to it, but asked me why I wanted to know. I told him that I was not only the Guard who handcuffed him a couple days ago, but I was also Broadbent's Brother in law, if he wanted to act the fool today I would welcome the challenge of coming in to his cell.

I/M Browning was quiet for the rest of the night.

Brothers and Sisters

Nothing in my story is unusual, heroic, or all that different from what hundreds of thousands of guards have been through. If I made it sound otherwise it is because of my Irish story telling DNA.

Watch your back, watch your partner's back.

We all gave some, some have given all.

Semper Vigilans.

Made in the USA
Middletown, DE
08 April 2018